CONTENTS

INTRODUCTION

An air fryer oven is a full-sized oven that features an air fry cooking mode integrated within the oven cavity. With this innovative technology, you can now enjoy all of the benefits of air fry no matter what kind of range you're looking for - induction, gas, or electric. By using a high-powered fan to circulate hot air around the food at a high speed, our in-range air fry feature cooks ingredients to a perfectly crisped finish.

The Benefits of an Air Frying Oven

An air frying oven uses little to no oil to create a flavorful and crunchy texture on foods and boasts all of the same benefits as a standalone air fryer - with some additional conveniences.

1. The air fry feature is integrated right into your oven, eliminating the need to store an extra appliance or take up valuable counter space.
2. An air frying oven has more capacity, saving you time and allowing you to cook more food at once so that there's always enough for the whole family.
3. A Frigidaire Air Fry Oven does more than just air fry, so one appliance works harder for you. Enjoy other features such as Even Baking with True Convection, Fast Steam Cleaning, and Smudge-Proof® Stainless Steel.

What Foods Can You Cook in an Air Frying Oven?

An air fryer oven does a delicious job at cooking most traditional deep-fried foods and these are some of our favorites:

- Sweet Potato or French fries
- Chicken wings or tenders
- Zucchini fries
- Onion rings
- Pepperoni pizza rolls
- Mac 'n' cheese
- Brussel sprouts

How do I keep my air frying oven clean?

Before using the air fry feature, place a cookie or baking sheet a rack or two under the Air Fry Tray to catch crumbs or drips. This will keep the bottom of the oven clean and free of fallen bits that can burn or cause odors later. Remember, do not place pans directly on the oven bottom to keep heat circulating correctly.

How do I clean the Air Fry Tray?

The Air Fry Tray is dishwasher safe, but for optimal cleaning, we recommend washing it by hand. It's designed to hold foods that already have some oil on them, which should keep food from sticking.

How do I limit the amount of smoke when using the Air Fry Tray?

Air fry uses really hot air to cook food fast and make it crunchy. Although air fry uses hot air to cook, remember that you are still frying your food so that it gets crispy! When some high-fat or greasy foods (like fresh wings) meet that hot air inside an oven, some smoke is normal. **If air fry is making a lot of smoke, try these tips:**

- When using the Air Fry Tray, put a baking sheet on a rack or two below the Air Fry Tray. This keeps drips and crumbs from landing on the oven bottom, where they can burn and create smoke. For additional protection, place some foil-lined parchment paper on the baking sheet. Parchment paper traps oil and keeps it from smoking.

- Use cooking oils that can stand up to high temperatures like avocado, grapeseed, and peanut oils. Cooking sprays made from these oils are available at the grocery store.

- Keep foil, parchment paper, and bakeware off the bottom of the oven. The oven bottom needs to stay clear so air can circulate.

- Don't overcrowd the food on your baking sheet or on the Air Fry Tray. If air can't circulate around each item, the cooking and crisping process may slow down and allow more grease to settle or drip.

- If your catch-tray is smoking, try placing parchment paper on it to hold grease. For extra-moist foods, you may have to use more. It's worth it!

- Some foods, like fresh wings and some vegetables, have a lot of moisture and may drip more than you expect. For items that might drip, use a pan with low sides if you're not using an Air Fry Tray.

- Air fry uses super-heated air, so if your oven bottom already has drips or crumbs on it (it happens!), those can smoke. Keep your oven bottom clean.

- If you have an oven vent, use it when cooking with air fry, like you would when using the cooktop.

MEAT RECIPES

Stuffed Pork Roll

Servings: 4
Cooking Time: 20 Minutes

Ingredients:
- 1 scallion, chopped
- ¼ cup sun-dried tomatoes, chopped finely
- 2 tablespoons fresh parsley, chopped
- Salt and freshly ground black pepper, to taste
- 4 (6-ounce) pork cutlets, pounded slightly
- 2 teaspoons paprika
- ½ tablespoons olive oil

Directions:
1. In a bowl, mix together the scallion, tomatoes, parsley, salt, and black pepper.
2. Spread the tomato mixture over each pork cutlet.
3. Roll each cutlet and secure with cocktail sticks.
4. Rub the outer part of rolls with paprika, salt and black pepper.
5. Coat the rolls with oil evenly.
6. Press "Power Button" of Ninja Foodi Digital Air Fry Oven and turn the dial to select "Air Fry" mode.
7. Press "Time Button" and again turn the dial to set the cooking time to 15 minutes.
8. Now push "Temp Button" and rotate the dial to set the temperature at 390 degrees F.
9. Press "Start/Pause" button to start.
10. When the unit beeps to show that it is preheated, open the lid and grease air fry basket.
11. Arrange pork rolls into the prepared air fry basket in a single layer and insert in the oven.
12. When cooking time is complete, open the lid and transfer the pork rolls onto serving plates.
13. Serve hot.
14. Serving Suggestions: Serve these pork rolls with creamed spinach.
15. Variation Tip: Drain the sun-dried tomatoes completely before using them.

Nutrition:
- Info Calories: 244 Fat: 14.5g Sat Fat: 2.7g Carbohydrates: 20.1g Fiber: 2.6g Sugar: 1.7g Protein: 8.2g

Braised Lamb Shanks

Servings: 4
Cooking Time: 2 Hours, 30 Minutes

Ingredients:

- 4 lamb shanks
- 4 crushed garlic cloves
- 2 tablespoons of olive oil
- 3 cups of beef broth
- 2 tablespoons balsamic vinegar

Directions:

1. Rub pepper and salt on your lamb shanks. Keep in the baking pan.
2. Rub the smashed garlic on the lamb well.
3. Now cut the shanks with olive oil.
4. Keep underneath your lamb.
5. Keep the pan into the rack.
6. Roast for 20 minutes at 425 degrees F. Change to low for 2 hours at 250 F.
7. Add vinegar and 2 cups of broth.
8. Including the remaining broth after the 1st hour.

Nutrition:

- Info Calories 453, Carbohydrates 6g, Cholesterol 121mg, Total Fat 37g, Protein 24g, Fiber 2g, Sodium 578mg

Sweet Potato, Brown Rice, And Lamb

Servings: 2
Cooking Time: 10 Minutes

Ingredients:
- ¼ cup lamb, cooked and puréed
- ½ cup cooked brown rice
- ¼ cup of sweet potato purée

Directions:
1. Keep all the ingredients in your bowl.
2. Pulse until you achieve the desired consistency.
3. Process with milk to get a smoother consistency.
4. Store in an airtight container. Refrigerate.

Nutrition:
- Info Calories 37, Carbohydrates 5g, Cholesterol 7mg, Total Fat 1g, Protein 2g, Fiber 1g, Sodium 6mg

Pork Skewers With Mango Salsa & Black Bean

Servings: 4

Cooking Time: 10 Minutes

Ingredients:
- 1 lb. pork tenderloin, cut into small cubes
- ½ can black beans, rinsed and drained
- 1 mango, peeled, seeded, and chopped
- 4-1/2 teaspoons of onion powder
- 4-1/2 teaspoons thyme, crushed
- 1 tablespoon vegetable oil
- ¼ teaspoon cloves, ground

Directions:
1. Stir in the thyme, onion powder, salt, and cloves in a bowl to create the seasoning mixture.
2. Keep a tablespoon of this for the pork. Transfer the remaining to an airtight container for later.
3. Preheat your air fryer to 175 degrees C or 350 degrees F.
4. Thread the chunks of pork into the skewers.
5. Brush oil on the pork. Sprinkle the seasoning mix on all sides.
6. Keep in your air fryer basket.
7. Cook for 5 minutes.
8. Mash one-third of the mango in your bowl in the meantime.
9. Stir the remaining mango in, and also salt, pepper, and black beans.
10. Serve the salsa with the pork skewers.

Nutrition:
- Info Calories 372, Carbohydrates 35g, Cholesterol 49mg, Total Fat 16g, Fiber 7g, Protein 22g, Sugar 18g, Sodium 1268mg

Almonds Crusted Rack Of Lamb

Servings: 5

Cooking Time: 35 Minutes

Ingredients:

- 1 tablespoon olive oil
- 1 garlic clove, minced
- Salt and freshly ground black pepper, to taste
- 1 (1¾-pound) rack of lamb
- 1 egg
- 1 tablespoon breadcrumbs
- 3 ounces almonds, finely chopped

Directions:

1. In a bowl, mix together the oil, garlic, salt, and black pepper.
2. Coat the rack of lamb evenly with oil mixture.
3. Crack the egg in a shallow bowl and beat well.
4. In another bowl, mix together the breadcrumbs and almonds.
5. Dip the rack of lamb in beaten egg and then, coat with almond mixture.
6. Press "Power Button" of Ninja Foodi Digital Air Fry Oven and turn the dial to select "Air Fry" mode.
7. Press "Time Button" and again turn the dial to set the cooking time to 30 minutes.
8. Now push "Temp Button" and rotate the dial to set the temperature at 220 degrees F.
9. Press "Start/Pause" button to start.
10. When the unit beeps to show that it is preheated, open the lid and grease air fry basket.
11. Place the rack of lamb into the prepared air fry basket and insert in the oven.
12. After 30 minutes, set the temperature of to 390 degrees F for 5 minutes.
13. When cooking time is complete, open the lid and place the rack of lamb onto a cutting board for about 5 minutes.
14. With a sharp knife, cut the rack of lamb into individual chops and serve.
15. Serving Suggestions: Serve with a fresh spinach salad.
16. Variation Tip: For best result, remove the silver skin from rack of lamb.

Nutrition:

- Info Calories: 408 Fat: 26.3g Sat Fat: 6.3g Carbohydrates: 4.9g Fiber: 2.2g Sugar: 0.9g Protein: 37.2g

Air-fried Meatloaf

Servings: 4
Cooking Time: 45 Minutes

Ingredients:

- 8 oz. pork, ground
- 8 oz. veal, ground
- 1 large egg
- ¼ cup bread crumbs
- 1.4 cup cilantro, chopped
- 1 teaspoon of olive oil
- 2 teaspoons chipotle chili sauce

Directions:

1. Preheat your air fryer to 200 degrees C or 400 degrees F.
2. Bring together the veal and pork in a baking dish. Make sure that it goes into your air fryer basket.
3. Create a well. Now add the cilantro, egg, bread crumbs, salt, and pepper.
4. Use your hands to mix well and create a loaf.
5. Combine the olive oil and chipotle chili sauce in a bowl. Whisk well.
6. Keep it aside.
7. Cook the meatloaf in your air fryer. Take it out and add the juicy mix.
8. Bring back the meatloaf to the fryer. Bake for 7 minutes.
9. Turn the fryer off. Allow the meatloaf to rest for 6 minutes inside.
10. Take it out and let it rest for 5 more minutes.
11. Slice before serving.

Nutrition:

- Info Calories 311, Carbohydrates 13g, Cholesterol 123mg, Total Fat 19g, Fiber 0.7g, Protein 22g, Sugar 8g, Sodium 536mg

Pork Meatloaf

Servings: 8
Cooking Time: 1 Hour 5 Minutes

Ingredients:

- For Meatloaf:
- 2 pounds lean ground pork
- 1 cup quick-cooking oats
- ½ cup carrot, peeled and shredded
- 1 medium onion, chopped
- ½ cup fat-free milk
- ¼ of egg, beaten
- 2 tablespoons ketchup
- 1 teaspoon garlic powder
- ¼ teaspoon ground black pepper
- For Topping:
- ¼ cup ketchup
- ¼ cup quick-cooking oats

Directions:

1. For meatloaf: in a bowl, add all the ingredients and mix until well combined.
2. For topping: in another bowl, add all the ingredients and mix until well combined.
3. Transfer the mixture into a greased loaf pan and top with the topping mixture.
4. Press "Power Button" of Ninja Foodi Digital Air Fry Oven and turn the dial to select "Air Bake" mode.
5. Press "Time Button" and again turn the dial to set the cooking time to 65 minutes.
6. Now push "Temp Button" and rotate the dial to set the temperature at 350 degrees F.
7. Press "Start/Pause" button to start.
8. When the unit beeps to show that it is preheated, open the lid.
9. Arrange the loaf pan over the wire rack and insert in the oven.
10. When cooking time is complete, open the lid and place the loaf pan onto a wire rack for about 10 minutes.
11. Carefully invert the loaf onto the wire rack.
12. Cut into desired sized slices and serve.
13. Serving Suggestions: Baked cauliflower will nicely accompany this meatloaf.
14. Variation Tip: Add in a sprinkling of Italian seasoning in meatloaf.

Nutrition:

- Info Calories: 239 Fat: 9.1g Sat Fat: 2.7g Carbohydrates: 14.5g Fiber: 1.8g Sugar: 4.5g Protein: 25.1g

Italian-style Meatballs

Servings: 12
Cooking Time: 35 Minutes

Ingredients:
- 10 oz. lean beef, ground
- 3 garlic cloves, minced
- 5 oz. turkey sausage
- 2 tablespoons shallot, minced
- 1 large egg, lightly beaten
- 2 tablespoons of olive oil
- 1 tablespoon of rosemary and thyme, chopped

Directions:
1. Preheat your air fryer to 400 degrees F.
2. Heat oil and add the shallot. Cook for 1-2 minutes.
3. Add the garlic now and cook. Take out from the heat.
4. Add the garlic and cooked shallot along with the egg, turkey sausage, beef, rosemary, thyme, and salt. Combine well by stirring.
5. Shape the mixture gently into 1-1/2 inch small balls.
6. Keep the balls in your air fryer basket.
7. Cook your meatballs at 400 degrees F. They should turn light brown.
8. Take out. Keep warm.
9. Serve the meatballs over rice or pasta.

Nutrition:
- Info Calories 175, Carbohydrates 0g, Total Fat 15g, Fiber 0g, Protein 10g, Sugar 0g, Sodium 254mg

Beef Kabobs

Servings: 4
Cooking Time: 10 Minutes

Ingredients:

- 1 oz. beef ribs, cut into small 1-inch pieces
- 2 tablespoons soy sauce
- 1/3 cup low-fat sour cream
- 1 bell pepper
- ½ onion

Directions:

1. Mix soy sauce and sour cream in a bowl.
2. Keep the chunks of beef in the bowl. Marinate for 30 minutes' minimum.
3. Now cut the onion and bell pepper into one-inch pieces.
4. Soak 8 skewers in water.
5. Thread the bell pepper, onions, and beef on the skewers. Add some pepper.
6. Cook for 10 minutes in your pre-heated air fryer. Turn after 5 minutes.

Nutrition:

- Info Calories 297, Carbohydrates 4g, Cholesterol 84mg, Total Fat 21g, Protein 23g, Sugar 2g, Sodium 609mg, Calcium 49mg

Rosemary Garlic Lamb Chops

Servings: 2

Cooking Time: 12 Minutes

Ingredients:

- 4 chops of lamb
- 1 teaspoon olive oil
- 2 teaspoon garlic puree
- Fresh garlic
- Fresh rosemary

Directions:

1. Keep your lamb chops in the fryer grill pan.
2. Season the chops with pepper and salt. Brush some olive oil.
3. Add some garlic puree on each chop.
4. Cover the grill pan gaps with garlic cloves and rosemary sprigs.
5. Refrigerate the grill pan to marinate.
6. Take out after 1 hour. Keep in the fryer and cook for 5 minutes.
7. Use your spatula to turn the chops over.
8. Add some olive oil and cook for another 5 minutes.
9. Set aside for a minute.
10. Take out the rosemary and garlic before serving.

Nutrition:

- Info Calories 678, Carbohydrates 1g, Cholesterol 257mg, Total Fat 38g, Protein 83g, Sugar 0g, Sodium 200mg

Glazed Lamb Meatballs

Servings: 8
Cooking Time: 30 Minutes

Ingredients:
- For Meatballs:
- 2 pounds lean ground lamb
- 2/3 cup quick-cooking oats
- ½ cup Ritz crackers, crushed
- 1 (5-ounce) can evaporated milk
- 2 large eggs, beaten lightly
- 1 teaspoon maple syrup
- 1 tablespoon dried onion, minced
- Salt and freshly ground black pepper, to taste
- For Sauce:
- 1/3 cup orange marmalade
- 1/3 cup maple syrup
- 1/3 cup sugar
- 2 tablespoons cornstarch
- 2 tablespoons soy sauce
- 1-2 tablespoons Sriracha
- 1 tablespoon Worcestershire sauce

Directions:

1. For meatballs: in a large bowl, add all the ingredients and mix until well combined.
2. Make 1½-inch balls from the mixture.
3. Arrange half of the meatballs onto the greased sheet pan in a single layer.
4. Press "Power Button" of Ninja Foodi Digital Air Fry Oven and turn the dial to select "Air Fry" mode.
5. Press "Time Button" and again turn the dial to set the cooking time to 15 minutes.
6. Now push "Temp Button" and rotate the dial to set the temperature at 380 degrees F.
7. Press "Start/Pause" button to start.
8. When the unit beeps to show that it is preheated, open the lid and insert the sheet pan in the oven.
9. Flip the meatballs once halfway through.
10. When cooking time is complete, open the lid and transfer the meatballs into a bowl.
11. Repeat with the remaining meatballs.
12. Meanwhile, for sauce: in a small pan, add all the ingredients over medium heat and cook until thickened, stirring continuously.
13. Serve the meatballs with the topping of sauce.
14. Serving Suggestions: Mashed buttery potatoes make a classic pairing with meatballs.
15. Variation Tip: You can adjust the ratio of sweetener according to your taste.

Nutrition:

- Info Calories: 413, Fat: 11.9g, Sat Fat: 4.3g Carbohydrates: 39.5g, Fiber: 1g Sugar: 28.2g, Protein: 36.2g

Buttered Rib Eye Steak

Servings: 3
Cooking Time: 14 Minutes

Ingredients:

- 2 (8-ounce) rib eye steaks
- 2 tablespoons butter, melted
- Salt and ground black pepper, as required

Directions:

1. Coat the steak with butter and then, sprinkle with salt and black pepper evenly.
2. Press "Power Button" of Ninja Foodi Digital Air Fry Oven and turn the dial to select the "Air Roast" mode.
3. Press the Time button and again turn the dial to set the cooking time to 14 minutes.
4. Now push the Temp button and rotate the dial to set the temperature at 400 degrees F.
5. Press "Start/Pause" button to start.
6. When the unit beeps to show that it is preheated, open the lid and grease "Air Fry Basket".
7. Arrange the steaks into "Air Fry Basket" and insert in the oven.
8. Remove from the oven and place steaks onto a platter for about 5 minutes.
9. Cut each steak into desired size slices and serve.

Nutrition:

- Info Calories 388 Total Fat 23.7 g Saturated Fat 110.2 g Cholesterol 154 mg Sodium 278 mg Total Carbs 0 g Fiber 0 g Sugar 0 g Protein 41 g

Herbed Pork Chops

Servings: 3
Cooking Time: 12 Minutes

Ingredients:

- 2 garlic cloves, minced
- ½ tablespoons fresh cilantro, chopped
- ½ tablespoons fresh rosemary, chopped
- ½ tablespoons fresh parsley, chopped
- 2 tablespoons olive oil
- ¾ tablespoons Dijon mustard
- 1 tablespoon ground coriander
- 1 teaspoon sugar
- Salt, to taste
- 3 (6-ounce) (1-inch thick) pork chops

Directions:

1. In a bowl, mix together the garlic, herbs, oil, mustard, coriander, sugar, and salt.
2. Add the pork chops and coat with marinade generously.
3. Cover the bowl and refrigerate for about 2-3 hours.
4. Remove chops from the refrigerator and set aside at room temperature for about 30 minutes.
5. Press "Power Button" of Ninja Foodi Digital Air Fry Oven and turn the dial to select "Air Fry" mode.
6. Press "Time Button" and again turn the dial to set the cooking time to 12 minutes.
7. Now push "Temp Button" and rotate the dial to set the temperature at 390 degrees F.
8. Press "Start/Pause" button to start.
9. When the unit beeps to show that it is preheated, open the lid and grease the air fry basket.
10. Arrange chops into the prepared Air Fryer basket in a single layer and insert in the oven.
11. When cooking time is complete, open the lid and transfer the chops onto plates.
12. Serve hot.
13. Serving Suggestions: Serve thee chops with curried potato salad.
14. Variation Tip: Bring the pork chops to room temperature before cooking.

Nutrition:

- Info Calories: 341 Fat: 25.5g Sat Fat: 6.8g Carbohydrates: 2.9g Fiber: 0.4g Sugar: 1.4g Protein: 32.3g

Seasoned Sirloin Steak

Servings: 2
Cooking Time: 12 Minutes

Ingredients:

- 2 (7-ounce) top sirloin steak
- 1 tablespoon steak seasoning
- Salt and ground black pepper, as required

Directions:

1. Season each steak with steak seasoning, salt and black pepper.
2. Arrange the steaks onto the greased cooking pan.
3. Press "Power Button" of Ninja Foodi Digital Air Fry Oven and turn the dial to select the "Air Fry" mode.
4. Press the Time button and again turn the dial to set the cooking time to 12 minutes.
5. Now push the Temp button and rotate the dial to set the temperature at 400 degrees F.
6. Press "Start/Pause" button to start.
7. When the unit beeps to show that it is preheated, open the lid and insert baking pan in the oven.
8. Flip the steaks once halfway through.
9. Remove from oven and serve.

Nutrition:

- Info Calories 369 Total Fat 12.4 g Saturated Fat 4.7 g Cholesterol 177 mg Sodium 208 mg Total Carbs 0 g Fiber 0 g Sugar 0 g Protein 60.2 g

Spiced Pork Shoulder

Servings: 6
Cooking Time: 55 Minutes

Ingredients:

- 1 teaspoon ground cumin
- 1 teaspoon cayenne pepper
- ½ teaspoon garlic powder
- ½ teaspoon onion powder
- Salt and ground black pepper, as required
- 2 pounds skin-on pork shoulder

Directions:

1. In a small bowl, place the spices, salt and black pepper and mix well.
2. Arrange the pork shoulder onto a cutting board, skin-side down.
3. Season the inner side of pork shoulder with salt and black pepper.
4. With kitchen twines, tie the pork shoulder into a long round cylinder shape.
5. Season the outer side of pork shoulder with spice mixture.
6. Press "Power Button" of Ninja Foodi Digital Air Fry Oven and turn the dial to select the "Air Roast" mode.
7. Press the Time button and again turn the dial to set the cooking time to 55 minutes.
8. Now push the Temp button and rotate the dial to set the temperature at 350 degrees F.
9. Press "Start/Pause" button to start.
10. When the unit beeps to show that it is preheated, open the lid and grease "Air Fry Basket".
11. Arrange the pork shoulder into "Air Fry Basket" and insert in the oven.
12. Remove from oven and place the pork shoulder onto a platter for about 10 minutes before slicing.
13. With a sharp knife, cut the pork shoulder into desired sized slices and serve.

Nutrition:

- Info Calories 445 Total Fat 32.5 g Saturated Fat 11.9 g Cholesterol 136 mg Sodium 131 mg Total Carbs 0.7 g Fiber 0.2 g Sugar 0.2 g Protein 35.4 g

Simple Beef Tenderloin

Servings: 10
Cooking Time: 50 Minutes

Ingredients:

- 1 (3½-pound) beef tenderloin, trimmed
- 2 tablespoons olive oil
- Salt and ground black pepper, as required

Directions:

1. With kitchen twine, tie the tenderloin.
2. Rub the tenderloin with oil and season with salt and black pepper.
3. Place the tenderloin into the greased baking pan.
4. Press "Power Button" of Ninja Foodi Digital Air Fry Oven and turn the dial to select the "Air Roast" mode.
5. Press the Time button and again turn the dial to set the cooking time to 50 minutes.
6. Now push the Temp button and rotate the dial to set the temperature at 400 degrees F.
7. Press "Start/Pause" button to start.
8. When the unit beeps to show that it is preheated, open the lid and insert baking pan in the oven.
9. Remove from oven and place the tenderloin onto a platter for about 10 minutes before slicing.
10. With a sharp knife, cut the tenderloin into desired sized slices and serve.

Nutrition:

- Info Calories 351 Total Fat 17.3 g Saturated Fat 5.9 g Cholesterol 146 mg Sodium 109 mg Total Carbs 0 g Fiber 0 g Sugar 0 g Protein 46 g

VEGETARIAN AND VEGAN RECIPES

Sweet & Tangy Mushrooms

Servings: 4
Cooking Time: 15 Minutes

Ingredients:

- ¼ cup soy sauce
- ¼ cup honey
- ¼ cup balsamic vinegar
- 2 garlic cloves, chopped finely
- ½ teaspoon red pepper flakes, crushed
- 18 ounces cremini mushrooms, halved

Directions:

1. In a bowl, place the soy sauce, honey, vinegar, garlic and red pepper flakes and mix well. Set aside.
2. Place the mushroom into the greased baking pan in a single layer.
3. Press "Power Button" of Ninja Foodi Digital Air Fry Oven and turn the dial to select the "Air Bake" mode.
4. Press the Time button and again turn the dial to set the cooking time to 15 minutes.
5. Now push the Temp button and rotate the dial to set the temperature at 350 degrees F.
6. Press "Start/Pause" button to start.
7. When the unit beeps to show that it is preheated, open the lid.
8. Insert the baking pan in oven.
9. After 8 minutes of cooking, place the honey mixture in baking pan and toss to coat well.
10. Serve hot.

Nutrition:

- Info Calories 113 Total Fat 0.2 g Saturated Fat 0 g Cholesterol 0 mg Sodium 9.8 mg Total Carbs 24.7 g Fiber 1 g Sugar 20 g Protein 4.4 g

Potato Gratin

Servings: 4
Cooking Time: 20 Minutes

Ingredients:
- 2 large potatoes, sliced thinly
- 5½ tablespoons cream
- 2 eggs
- 1 tablespoon plain flour
- ½ cup cheddar cheese, grated

Directions:
1. Press "Power Button" of Ninja Foodi Digital Air Fry Oven and turn the dial to select "Air Fry" mode.
2. Press "Time Button" and again turn the dial to set the cooking time to 10 minutes.
3. Now push "Temp Button" and rotate the dial to set the temperature at 355 degrees F.
4. Press "Start/Pause" button to start.
5. When the unit beeps to show that it is preheated, open the lid.
6. Arrange the potato slices in the air fry basket and insert in the oven.
7. Meanwhile, in a bowl, add cream, eggs and flour and mix until a thick sauce forms.
8. When cooking time is complete, open the lid and remove the potato slices from the basket.
9. Divide the potato slices in 4 ramekins evenly and top with the egg mixture evenly, followed by the cheese.
10. Press "Power Button" of Ninja Foodi Digital Air Fry Oven and turn the dial to select "Air Fry" mode.
11. Press "Time Button" and again turn the dial to set the cooking time to 10 minutes.
12. Now push "Temp Button" and rotate the dial to set the temperature at 390 degrees F.
13. Arrange the ramekins in the air fry basket and insert in the oven.
14. Press "Start/Pause" button to start.
15. When cooking time is complete, open the lid and remove the ramekins from the oven.
16. Serve warm.
17. Serving Suggestions: Serve this gratin with fresh lettuce.
18. Variation Tip: Make sure to cut the potato slices thinly.

Nutrition:
- Info Calories: 233 Fat: 8g Sat Fat: 4.3g Carbohydrates: 31.3g Fiber: 4.5g Sugar: 2.7g Protein: 9.7g

Veggie Kabobs

Servings: 6
Cooking Time: 10 Minutes

Ingredients:

- ¼ cup carrots, peeled and chopped
- ¼ cup French beans
- ½ cup green peas
- 1 teaspoon ginger
- 3 garlic cloves, peeled
- 3 green chilies
- ¼ cup fresh mint leaves
- ½ cup cottage cheese
- 2 medium boiled potatoes, mashed
- ½ teaspoon five-spice powder
- Salt, to taste
- 2 tablespoons corn flour
- Olive oil cooking spray

Directions:

1. In a food processor, add the carrot, beans, peas, ginger, garlic, mint, cheese and pulse until smooth.
2. Transfer the mixture into a bowl.
3. Add the mashed potatoes, five-spice powder, salt and corn flour and with your hands mix until well combined.
4. Shape the mixture into equal-sized small balls.
5. Press each ball around a skewer in a sausage shape.
6. Spray the skewers with cooking spray.
7. Press "Power Button" of Ninja Foodi Digital Air Fry Oven and turn the dial to select "Air Fry" mode.
8. Press "Time Button" and again turn the dial to set the cooking time to 10 minutes.
9. Now push "Temp Button" and rotate the dial to set the temperature at 390 degrees F.
10. Press "Start/Pause" button to start.
11. When the unit beeps to show that it is preheated, open the lid and grease the air fry basket.
12. Arrange the skewers into the prepared air fry basket and insert in the oven.
13. When cooking time is complete, open the lid and transfer the skewers onto a platter.
14. Serve warm.
15. Serving Suggestions: Enjoy these kabobs wt yogurt dip.
16. Variation Tip: You can add spices of your choice in these veggie kabobs

Nutrition:

- Info Calories: 120, Fat: 0.8g Sat Fat: 0.3g, Carbohydrates: 21.9g Fiber: 4.9g Sugar: 1.8g Protein: 6.3g

Roasted Vegetables

Servings: 4

Cooking Time: 20 Minutes

Ingredients:

- 1 yellow squash, cut into small pieces
- 1 red bell pepper, seeded and cut into small pieces
- ¼ oz. mushrooms, cleaned and halved
- 1 tablespoon of extra-virgin olive oil
- 1 zucchini, cut into small pieces

Directions:

1. Preheat your air fryer. Keep the squash, red bell pepper, and mushrooms in a bowl.

2. Add the black pepper, salt, and olive oil. Combine well by tossing.

3. Keep the vegetables in your fryer basket.

4. Air fry them for 15 minutes. They should get roasted. Stir about halfway into the roasting time.

Nutrition:

- Info Calories 89, Carbohydrates 8g, Cholesterol 0mg, Total Fat 5g, Protein 3g, Sugar 4g, Fiber 2.3g, Sodium 48mg

Green Beans & Mushroom Casserole

Servings: 6
Cooking Time: 12 Minutes

Ingredients:

- 24 ounces fresh green beans, trimmed
- 2 cups fresh button mushrooms, sliced
- 3 tablespoons olive oil
- 2 tablespoons fresh lemon juice
- 1 teaspoon ground sage
- 1 teaspoon garlic powder
- 1 teaspoon onion powder
- Salt and freshly ground black pepper, to taste
- 1/3 cup French fried onions

Directions:

1. In a bowl, add the green beans, mushrooms, oil, lemon juice, sage, and spices and toss to coat well.
2. Press "Power Button" of Ninja Foodi Digital Air Fry Oven and turn the dial to select "Air Fry" mode.
3. Press "Time Button" and again turn the dial to set the cooking time to 12 minutes.
4. Now push "Temp Button" and rotate the dial to set the temperature at 400 degrees F.
5. Press "Start/Pause" button to start.
6. When the unit beeps to show that it is preheated, open the lid and grease the air fry basket.
7. Arrange the mushroom mixture into the prepared air fry basket and insert in the oven.
8. Shake the mushroom mixture occasionally.
9. When cooking time is complete, open the lid and transfer the mushroom mixture into a serving dish.
10. Top with fried onions and serve.
11. Serving Suggestions: Fresh salad will accompany this casserole nicely.
12. Variation Tip: Any kind of fresh mushrooms can be used.

Nutrition:

- Info Calories: 125 Fat: 8.6g Sat Fat: 2g Carbohydrates: 11g Fiber: 4.2g Sugar: 2.4g Protein: 3g

Sweet Potato Hash

Servings: 6
Cooking Time: 15 Minutes

Ingredients:

- 2 sweet potatoes, cubed into small pieces
- 2 tablespoons of olive oil
- 1 teaspoon black pepper, ground
- 1 tablespoon of smoked paprika
- 1 teaspoon dill weed, dried

Directions:

1. Preheat your air fryer to 200 degrees C or 400 degrees F.
2. Toss the olive oil, sweet potatoes, paprika, pepper, and salt in a bowl.
3. Keep this mixture in your air fryer.
4. Now cook for 12 minutes.
5. Check first, and then stir after 8 minutes. Stir after another 2 minutes. It should turn brown and crispy.

Nutrition:

- Info Calories 203, Carbohydrates 31g, Cholesterol 3mg, Total Fat 7g, Protein 4g, Sugar 6g, Fiber 5g, Sodium 447mg

Glazed Mushrooms

Servings: 4
Cooking Time: 15 Minutes

Ingredients:
- ¼ cup soy sauce
- ¼ cup honey
- ¼ cup balsamic vinegar
- 2 garlic cloves, chopped finely
- ½ teaspoon red pepper flakes, crushed
- 18 ounces fresh Cremini mushrooms, halved

Directions:
1. In a bowl, place the soy sauce, honey, vinegar, garlic and red pepper flakes and mix well. Set aside.
2. Place the mushroom into the greased baking pan in a single layer.
3. Press "Power Button" of Ninja Foodi Digital Air Fry Oven and turn the dial to select "Air Bake" mode.
4. Press "Time Button" and again turn the dial to set the cooking time to 15 minutes.
5. Now push "Temp Button" and rotate the dial to set the temperature at 350 degrees F.
6. Press "Start/Pause" button to start.
7. When the unit beeps to show that it is preheated, open the lid.
8. Insert the baking pan in oven.
9. After 8 minutes of cooking, place the honey mixture in baking pan and toss to coat well.
10. When cooking time is complete, open the lid and transfer the mushrooms onto serving plates.
11. Serve hot.
12. Serving Suggestions: Topping of fresh chives or marjoram gives a delish touch to mushrooms.
13. Variation Tip: Maple syrup will be an excellent substitute for honey.

Nutrition:
- Info Calories: 113 Fat: 0.2g Sat Fat: 0g Carbohydrates: 24.7g Fiber: 1g Sugar: 20g Protein: 4.4g

Tofu With Broccoli

Servings: 3
Cooking Time: 15 Minutes

Ingredients:
- 8 ounces firm tofu, drained, pressed and cubed
- 1 head broccoli, cut into florets
- 1 tablespoon butter, melted
- 1 teaspoon ground turmeric
- ¼ teaspoon paprika
- Salt and ground black pepper, as required

Directions:
1. In a bowl, mix together all ingredients.
2. Place the tofu mixture in the greased cooking pan.
3. Press "Power Button" of Ninja Foodi Digital Air Fry Oven and turn the dial to select the "Air Fry" mode.
4. Press the Time button and again turn the dial to set the cooking time to 15 minutes.
5. Now push the Temp button and rotate the dial to set the temperature at 390 degrees F.
6. Press "Start/Pause" button to start.
7. When the unit beeps to show that it is preheated, open the lid.
8. Insert the baking pan in oven.
9. Toss the tofu mixture once halfway through.
10. Serve hot.

Nutrition:
- Info Calories 119 Total Fat 7.4 g Saturated Fat 3.1 g Cholesterol 10 mg Sodium 115 mg Total Carbs 7.5 g Fiber 3.1 g Sugar 1.9 g Protein 8.7 g

Spicy Butternut Squash

Servings: 4
Cooking Time: 20 Minutes

Ingredients:

- 1 medium butternut squash, peeled, seeded and cut into chunk
- 2 teaspoons cumin seeds
- 1/8 teaspoon garlic powder
- 1/8 teaspoon chili flakes, crushed
- Salt and freshly ground black pepper, to taste
- 1 tablespoon olive oil
- 2 tablespoons pine nuts
- 2 tablespoons fresh cilantro, chopped

Directions:

1. In a bowl, mix together the squash, spices, and oil.
2. Press "Power Button" of Ninja Foodi Digital Air Fry Oven and turn the dial to select "Air Fry" mode.
3. Press "Time Button" and again turn the dial to set the cooking time to 20 minutes.
4. Now push "Temp Button" and rotate the dial to set the temperature at 375 degrees F.
5. Press "Start/Pause" button to start.
6. When the unit beeps to show that it is preheated, open the lid and grease the air fry basket.
7. Arrange the squash chunks into the prepared air fry basket and insert in the oven.
8. When cooking time is complete, open the lid and transfer the squash chunks onto serving plates.
9. Serve hot with the garnishing of pine nuts and cilantro.
10. Serving Suggestions: Serve with a sprinkle of sweet dried cranberries.
11. Variation Tip: you can microwave the butternut squash for 2-3 mins to make it softer and easier to remove the skin.

Nutrition:

- Info Calories: 191 Fat: 7g Sat Fat: 0.8g Carbohydrates: 34.3g Fiber: 6g Sugar: 6.4g Protein: 3.7g

Air Fryer Pumpkin Keto Pancakes

Servings: 2

Cooking Time: 5 Minutes

Ingredients:
- ½ cup pumpkin puree
- 1 teaspoon of vanilla extract
- 2 eggs
- ½ cup peanut butter
- ½ teaspoon baking soda

Directions:
1. Use parchment paper to line the basket of your air fryer.
2. Apply some cooking spray.
3. Bring together the eggs, peanut butter, pumpkin puree, baking soda, salt, and eggs in a bowl. Combine well by stirring.
4. Place 3 tablespoons of the batter in each pancake. There should be a half-inch space between them.
5. Keep the basket in your air fryer oven.
6. Cook for 4 minutes at 150 degrees C or 300 degrees F.

Nutrition:
- Info Calories 586, Carbohydrates 20g, Cholesterol 186mg, Total Fat 46g, Protein 23g, Sugar 9g, Fiber 6g, Sodium 906mg

Roasted Okra

Servings: 1
Cooking Time: 15 Minutes

Ingredients:

- ½ oz. okra, trimmed ends and sliced pods
- ¼ teaspoon salt
- 1 teaspoon olive oil
- 1/8 teaspoon black pepper, ground

Directions:

1. Preheat your air fryer to 175 degrees C or 350 degrees F.
2. Bring together the olive oil, okra, pepper, and salt in a mid-sized bowl.
3. Stir gently.
4. Keep in your air fryer basket. It should be in one single layer.
5. Cook for 5 minutes in the fryer. Toss once and cook for another 5 minutes.
6. Toss once more. Cook again for 2 minutes.

Nutrition:

- Info Calories 138, Carbohydrates 16g, Cholesterol 0mg, Total Fat 6g, Protein 5g, Sugar 3g, Fiber 7g, Sodium 600mg

Air-fried Italian-style Ratatouille

Servings: 4
Cooking Time: 25 Minutes

Ingredients:
- ½ eggplant, cubed into small pieces
- 1 medium-sized tomato, cubed
- 1 zucchini, cubed
- 2 oregano sprigs, stemmed and chopped
- 1 tablespoon olive oil
- 1 tablespoon of white wine

Directions:
1. Preheat your air fryer to 200 degrees C or 400 degrees F.
2. Place the zucchini, eggplant, and tomato in a bowl.
3. Now add the oregano, pepper, and salt.
4. Distribute well by mixing.
5. Drizzle in the white wine and oil. Coat the vegetables well.
6. Pour the vegetable mix into your baking dish.
7. Insert this into your air fryer basket.
8. Cook for 15 minutes, stirring once.
9. Stir once more and keep cooking until it gets tender.
10. Turn the air fryer off.
11. Let it rest for 5-7 minutes before serving.

Nutrition:
- Info Calories 93, Carbohydrates 10g, Cholesterol 0mg, Total Fat 5g, Protein 2g, Sugar 5g, Fiber 3g, Sodium 48mg

Fried Green Tomatoes

Servings: 6
Cooking Time: 20 Minutes

Ingredients:

- 2 tomatoes, cut into small slices
- ½ cup buttermilk
- 2 eggs, beaten lightly
- 1 cup bread crumbs
- 1/3 cup of all-purpose flour
- 1 cup yellow cornmeal

Directions:

1. Season the slices of tomato with pepper and salt.
2. Take 2 breeding dishes. Keep flour in the first, stir in eggs and buttermilk in the second, and mix cornmeal and bread crumbs in the third.
3. Dredge the slices of tomato in your flour. Shake off any excess.
4. Now dip the tomatoes in the egg mix.
5. Then dip into the bread crumb mix. Coat both sides.
6. Preheat your air fryer to 200 degrees C or 400 degrees F.
7. Brush olive oil on the fryer basket.
8. Keep the slices of tomato in your fryer basket. They shouldn't touch.
9. Brush some olive oil on the tomato tops.
10. Cook for 10 minutes. Flip your tomatoes, brush olive oil and cook for another 5 minutes.
11. Take the tomatoes out. Keep in a rack lined with a paper towel.

Nutrition:

- Info Calories 246, Carbohydrates 40g, Cholesterol 63mg, Total Fat 6g, Protein 8g, Sugar 3g, Fiber 2g, Sodium 166mg

Stuffed Zucchini

Servings: 4
Cooking Time: 35 Minutes

Ingredients:
- 2 zucchinis, cut in half lengthwise
- ½ teaspoon garlic powder
- Salt, as required
- 1 teaspoon olive oil
- 4 ounces fresh mushrooms, chopped
- 4 ounces carrots, peeled and shredded
- 3 ounces onion, chopped
- 4 ounces goat cheese, crumbled
- 12 fresh basil leaves
- ½ teaspoon onion powder

Directions:

1. Carefully, scoop the flesh from the middle of each zucchini half.
2. Season each zucchini half with a little garlic powder and salt.
3. Arrange the zucchini halves into the greased baking pan.
4. Place the oat mixture over salmon fillets and gently, press down.
5. Press "Power Button" of Ninja Foodi Digital Air Fry Oven and turn the dial to select the "Air Bake" mode.
6. Press the Time button and again turn the dial to set the cooking time to 20 minutes.
7. Now push the Temp button and rotate the dial to set the temperature at 450 degrees F.
8. Press "Start/Pause" button to start.
9. When the unit beeps to show that it is preheated, open the lid.
10. Insert the baking pan in oven.
11. Meanwhile, in a skillet, heat the oil over medium heat and cook the mushrooms, carrots, onions, onion powder and salt and cook for about 5-6 minutes.
12. Remove from the heat and set aside.
13. Remove the baking pan from oven and set aside.
14. Stuff each zucchini half with veggie mixture and top with basil leaves, followed by the cheese.
15. Press "Power Button" of Ninja Foodi Digital Air Fry Oven and turn the dial to select the "Air Bake" mode.
16. Press the Time button and again turn the dial to set the cooking time to 15 minutes.
17. Now push the Temp button and rotate the dial to set the temperature at 450 degrees F.
18. Press "Start/Pause" button to start.
19. When the unit beeps to show that it is preheated, open the lid.
20. Insert the baking pan in oven.

Nutrition:

- Info Calories 181 Total Fat 11.6 g Saturated Fat 7.2 g Cholesterol 30 mg Sodium 169 mg Total Carbs 10.1g Fiber 2.6 g Sugar 5.3 g Protein 11.3 g

Stuffed Pumpkin

Servings: 2

Cooking Time: 30 Minutes

Ingredients:

- ½ pumpkin, small
- 1 sweet potato, diced
- 1 parsnip, diced
- 1 carrot, diced
- 1 egg

Directions:

1. Scrape out the seeds from the pumpkin.
2. Combine the sweet potato, parsnip, carrot, and the egg in a bowl.
3. Fill up your pumpkin with this vegetable mixture.
4. Preheat your air fryer to 175 degrees C or 350 degrees F.
5. Keep your stuffed pumpkin in the fryer's basket.
6. Cook for 25 minutes. It should become tender.

Nutrition:

- Info Calories 268, Carbohydrates 49g, Cholesterol 93mg, Total Fat 4g, Protein 9g, Sugar 13g, Fiber 10g, Sodium 210mg

Broccoli With Cauliflower

Servings: 6
Cooking Time: 15 Minutes

Ingredients:

- 1-pound broccoli, cut into 1-inch florets
- 1-pound cauliflower, cut into 1-inch florets
- 2 tablespoons butter
- Salt and ground black pepper, as required
- ¼ cup Parmesan cheese, grated

Directions:

1. In a pan of the boiling water, add the broccoli and cook for about 3-4 minutes.
2. Drain the broccoli well.
3. In a bowl, place the broccoli, cauliflower, oil, salt, and black pepper and toss to coat well.
4. Press "Power Button" of Ninja Foodi Digital Air Fry Oven and turn the dial to select the "Air Fry" mode.
5. Press the Time button and again turn the dial to set the cooking time to 15 minutes.
6. Now push the Temp button and rotate the dial to set the temperature at 400 degrees F.
7. Press "Start/Pause" button to start.
8. When the unit beeps to show that it is preheated, open the lid.
9. Arrange the veggie mixture in "Air Fry Basket" and insert in the oven.
10. Toss the veggie mixture once halfway through.
11. Remove from oven and transfer the veggie mixture into a large bowl.
12. Immediately, stir in the cheese and serve immediately.

Nutrition:

- Info Calories 91 Total Fat 5 g Saturated Fat 2.8 g Cholesterol 13 mg Sodium 131 mg Total Carbs 9 g Fiber 3.9 g Sugar 3.1 g Protein 5 g

POULTRY RECIPES

Herbed Roasted Chicken

Servings: 6

Cooking Time: 1 Hour 10 Minutes

Ingredients:

- ¼ cup butter, softened
- 1 teaspoon dried rosemary, crushed
- 1 teaspoon dried basil, crushed
- 1 teaspoon dried oregano, crushed
- 1 teaspoon dried thyme, crushed
- 1 tablespoon garlic powder
- 1 tablespoon paprika
- 1 tablespoon ground cumin
- Salt and freshly ground black pepper, to taste
- 1 (3-pound) whole chicken, neck and giblets removed

Directions:

1. In a bowl, add the butter, herbs, spices and salt and mix well.
2. Rub the chicken with spice mixture generously.
3. With kitchen twine, tie off wings and legs.
4. Arrange the chicken onto the greased sheet pan.
5. Press "Power Button" of Ninja Foodi Digital Air Fry Oven and turn the dial to select "Air Bake" mode.
6. Press "Time Button" and again turn the dial to set the cooking time to 70 minutes.
7. Now push "Temp Button" and rotate the dial to set the temperature at 380 degrees F.
8. Press "Start/Pause" button to start.
9. When the unit beeps to show that it is preheated, open the lid and insert the sheet pan in oven.
10. When cooking time is complete, open the lid and place the chicken onto a platter for about 10-15 minutes before carving.
11. With a sharp knife, cut the chicken into desired sized pieces and serve.
12. Serving Suggestions: Roasted vegetables will accompany this roasted chicken nicely.
13. Variation Tip: Rub the chicken with your hands for even coating.

Nutrition:

- Info Calories: 434 Fat: 15g Sat Fat: 6.9g Carbohydrates: 2.5g Fiber: 0.9g Sugar: 0.5g Protein: 66.4g

Breaded Chicken Breast

Servings: 6
Cooking Time: 12 Minutes

Ingredients:

- 1 cup breadcrumbs
- ½ cup Parmesan cheese, grated
- ¼ cup fresh parsley, minced
- Salt and freshly ground black pepper, to taste
- 1½ pounds boneless, skinless chicken breasts
- 3 tablespoons olive oil
- Olive oil cooking spray

Directions:

1. In a shallow dish, add the breadcrumbs, Parmesan cheese, parsley, salt and black pepper mix well.
2. Rub the chicken breasts with oil and then, coat with the breadcrumbs mixture evenly.
3. Arrange the chicken breasts onto the sheet pan and spray with cooking spray.
4. Press "Power Button" of Ninja Foodi Digital Air Fry Oven and turn the dial to select "Air Fry" mode.
5. Press "Time Button" and again turn the dial to set the cooking time to 12 minutes.
6. Now push "Temp Button" and rotate the dial to set the temperature at 350 degrees F.
7. Press "Start/Pause" button to start.
8. When the unit beeps to show that it is preheated, open the lid and insert the sheet pan in the oven.
9. Flip the chicken breasts once halfway through.
10. When cooking time is complete, open the lid and transfer the chicken breasts onto a platter.
11. Serve hot.
12. Serving Suggestions: Enjoy these chicken breasts with honey mustard sauce.
13. Variation Tip: Pat dry the chicken breasts thoroughly before breading.

Nutrition:

- Info Calories: 371 Fat: 18g Sat Fat: 4.3g Carbohydrates: 13.1g Fiber: 0.9g Sugar: 1.1g Protein: 38g

Herbed & Spiced Turkey Breast

Servings: 6

Cooking Time: 40 Minutes

Ingredients:

- ¼ cup butter, softened
- 2 tablespoons fresh rosemary, chopped
- 2 tablespoon fresh thyme, chopped
- 2 tablespoons fresh sage, chopped
- 2 tablespoons fresh parsley, chopped
- Salt and ground black pepper, as required
- 1 (4-pound) bone-in, skin-on turkey breast
- 2 tablespoons olive oil

Directions:

1. In a bowl, add the butter, herbs, salt and black pepper and mix well.
2. Rub the herb mixture under skin evenly.
3. Coat the outside of turkey breast with oil.
4. Place the turkey breast into the greased baking pan.
5. Press "Power Button" of Ninja Foodi Digital Air Fry Oven and turn the dial to select the "Air Bake" mode.
6. Press the Time button and again turn the dial to set the cooking time to 40 minutes.
7. Now push the Temp button and rotate the dial to set the temperature at 350 degrees F.
8. Press "Start/Pause" button to start.
9. When the unit beeps to show that it is preheated, open the lid and insert baking pan in the oven.
10. Remove from oven and place the turkey breast onto a platter for about 5-10 minutes before slicing.
11. With a sharp knife, cut the turkey breast into desired sized slices and serve.

Nutrition:

- Info Calories 333 Total Fat 37 g Saturated Fat 12.4 g Cholesterol 209 mg Sodium 245 mg Total Carbs 1.8 g Fiber 1.1 g Sugar 0.1 g Protein 65.1 g

Turkey Breasts

Servings: 6
Cooking Time: 40 Minutes

Ingredients:
- 2-3/4 oz. turkey breasts, with skin
- 1 tablespoon rosemary, chopped
- 1 teaspoon chive, chopped
- 2 tablespoons of butter, unsalted
- 1 teaspoon garlic, minced

Directions:
1. Preheat your air fryer to 175 degrees C or 350 degrees F.
2. Keep the chives, rosemary, garlic, pepper, and salt on your cutting board.
3. Make thin slices of butter and place on the seasonings and herbs. Blend well.
4. Pat the herbed butter on both sides of the turkey breasts.
5. Keep the turkey in the air fryer basket, skin-down side.
6. Fry for 17 minutes.
7. Turn the skin-side up and keep frying for 8 more minutes at 74 degrees C or 165 degrees F.
8. Transfer to a plate. Set aside for 10 minutes.
9. Slice before serving.

Nutrition:
- Info Calories 287, Carbohydrates 0.3g, Cholesterol 86mg, Total Fat 14g, Protein 40g, Sugar 0g, Fiber 0.1g, Sodium 913mg

Spicy Chicken Legs

Servings: 6
Cooking Time: 25 Minutes

Ingredients:
- 2½ pounds chicken legs
- 2 tablespoons olive oil
- 1 teaspoon smoked paprika
- 1 teaspoon garlic powder
- ½ teaspoon ground cumin
- Salt and freshly ground black pepper, to taste

Directions:
1. In a large bowl, add all the ingredients and mix well.
2. Arrange the chicken legs onto a sheet pan.
3. Press "Power Button" of Ninja Foodi Digital Air Fry Oven and turn the dial to select "Air Fry" mode.
4. Press "Time Button" and again turn the dial to set the cooking time to 25 minutes.
5. Now push "Temp Button" and rotate the dial to set the temperature at 400 degrees F.
6. Press "Start/Pause" button to start.
7. When the unit beeps to show that it is preheated, open the lid and insert the sheet pan in the oven.
8. When cooking time is complete, open the lid and transfer the chicken legs onto serving plates.
9. Serve hot.
10. Serving Suggestions: Serve with cheesy baked asparagus.
11. Variation Tip: Don't accept any chicken legs that are soft and discolored.

Nutrition:
- Info Calories: 402 Fat: 18.8g Sat Fat: 4.5g Carbohydrates: 0.6g Fiber: 0.2g Sugar: 0.2g Protein: 54.8g

Air Fryer Chicken Wings

Servings: 4
Cooking Time: 30 Minutes

Ingredients:
- 1-1/2 oz. chicken wings
- 1 teaspoon garlic powder
- 1 teaspoon kosher salt
- 1 tablespoon of butter, unsalted and melted
- ½ cup hot sauce

Directions:
1. Keep your chicken wings in 1 layer. Use paper towels to pat them dry.
2. Sprinkle garlic powder and salt evenly.
3. Now keep these wings in your air fryer at 380°F.
4. Cook for 20 minutes. Toss after every 5 minutes. The wings should be cooked through and tender.
5. Bring up the temperature to 400 degrees F.
6. Cook for 5-8 minutes until it has turned golden brown and crispy.
7. Toss your wings with melted butter (optional) before serving.

Nutrition:
- Info Calories 291, Carbohydrates 1g, Total Fat 23g, Protein 20g, Sugar 0.3g, Fiber 0g, Sodium 593mg

Popcorn Chicken

Servings: 4

Cooking Time: 10 Minutes

Ingredients:
- 1 oz. chicken breast halves, boneless and skinless
- ½ teaspoon paprika
- ¼ teaspoon mustard, ground
- ¼ teaspoon of garlic powder
- 3 tablespoons of cornstarch

Directions:
1. Cut the chicken into small pieces and keep in a bowl.
2. Combine the paprika, garlic powder, mustard, salt, and pepper in another bowl.
3. Reserve a teaspoon of your seasoning mixture. Sprinkle the other portion on the chicken. Coat evenly by tossing.
4. Combine the reserved seasoning and cornstarch in a plastic bag.
5. Combine well by shaking.
6. Keep your chicken pieces in the bag. Seal it and shake for coating evenly.
7. Now transfer the chicken to a mesh strainer. Shake the excess cornstarch.
8. Keep aside for 5-10 minutes. The cornstarch should start to get absorbed into your chicken.
9. Preheat your air fryer to 200 degrees C or 390 degrees F.
10. Apply some oil on the air fryer basket.
11. Keep the chicken pieces inside. They should not overlap.
12. Apply cooking spray.
13. Cook until the chicken isn't pink anymore.

Nutrition:
- Info Calories 156, Carbohydrates 6g, Cholesterol 65mg, Total Fat 4g, Protein 24g, Sugar 0g, Fiber 0.3g, Sodium 493mg

Lemony Turkey Legs

Servings: 2
Cooking Time: 30 Minutes

Ingredients:

- 2 garlic cloves, minced
- 1 tablespoon fresh rosemary, minced
- 1 teaspoon fresh lemon zest, finely grated
- 2 tablespoons olive oil
- 1 tablespoon fresh lemon juice
- Salt and freshly ground black pepper, to taste
- 2 turkey legs

Directions:

1. In a large bowl, mix together the garlic, rosemary, lime zest, oil, lime juice, salt, and black pepper.
2. Add the turkey legs and coat with marinade generously.
3. Refrigerate to marinate for about 6-8 hours.
4. Press "Power Button" of Ninja Foodi Digital Air Fry Oven and turn the dial to select "Air Fry" mode.
5. Press "Time Button" and again turn the dial to set the cooking time to 30 minutes.
6. Now push "Temp Button" and rotate the dial to set the temperature at 350 degrees F.
7. Press "Start/Pause" button to start.
8. When the unit beeps to show that it is preheated, open the lid and grease the air fry basket.
9. Arrange the turkey legs into the prepared basket and insert in the oven.
10. Flip the turkey legs once halfway through.
11. When cooking time is complete, open the lid and transfer the turkey legs onto serving plates.
12. Serve hot.
13. Serving Suggestions: Serve these turkey legs with honey macadamia stuffing.
14. Variation Tip: A fresh turkey meat should never be chilled below 26 degrees.

Nutrition:

- Info Calories: 709 Fat: 32.7g Sat Fat: 7.8g Carbohydrates: 2.3g Fiber: 0.8g Sugar: 0.1g Protein: 97.2g

Roasted Cornish Game Hen

Servings: 4

Cooking Time: 16 Minutes

Ingredients:

- ¼ cup olive oil
- 1 teaspoon fresh rosemary, chopped
- 1 teaspoon fresh thyme, chopped
- 1 teaspoon fresh lemon zest, finely grated
- ¼ teaspoon sugar
- ¼ teaspoon red pepper flakes, crushed
- Salt and freshly ground black pepper, to taste
- 2 pounds Cornish game hen, backbone removed and halved

Directions:

1. In a bowl, mix together oil, herbs, lemon zest, sugar, and spices.
2. Add the hen portions and coat with the marinade generously.
3. Cover and refrigerate for about 24 hours.
4. In a strainer, place the hen portions and set aside to drain any liquid.
5. Press "Power Button" of Ninja Foodi Digital Air Fry Oven and turn the dial to select "Air Fry" mode.
6. Press "Time Button" and again turn the dial to set the cooking time to 16 minutes.
7. Now push "Temp Button" and rotate the dial to set the temperature at 390 degrees F.
8. Press "Start/Pause" button to start.
9. When the unit beeps to show that it is preheated, open the lid and grease the air fry basket.
10. Arrange the hen portions into the prepared basket and insert in the oven.
11. When cooking time is complete, open the lid and transfer the hen portions onto a platter.
12. Cut each portion in half and serve.
13. Serving Suggestions: Serve with dinner rolls.
14. Variation Tip: Place the hens in the basket, breast side up.

Nutrition:

- Info Calories: 557 Fat: 45.1g Sat Fat: 1.8g Carbohydrates: 0.8g Fiber: 0.3g Sugar: 0.3g Protein: 38.5g

Marinated Chicken Thighs

Servings: 4
Cooking Time: 30 Minutes

Ingredients:
- 4 (6-ounce) bone-in, skin-on chicken thighs
- Salt and freshly ground black pepper, to taste
- ½ cup Italian salad dressing
- 1 teaspoon onion powder
- 1 teaspoon garlic powder

Directions:
1. Season the chicken thighs with salt and black pepper evenly.
2. In a large bowl, add the chicken thighs and dressing and mix well.
3. Cover the bowl and refrigerate to marinate overnight.
4. Remove the chicken breast from the bowl and place onto a plate.
5. Sprinkle the chicken thighs with onion powder and garlic powder.
6. Press "Power Button" of Ninja Foodi Digital Air Fry Oven and turn the dial to select "Air Fry" mode.
7. Press "Time Button" and again turn the dial to set the cooking time to 30 minutes.
8. Now push "Temp Button" and rotate the dial to set the temperature at 360 degrees F.
9. Press "Start/Pause" button to start.
10. When the unit beeps to show that it is preheated, open the lid and grease the air fry basket.
11. Arrange the chicken thighs into the prepared basket and insert in the oven.
12. After 15 minutes of cooking, flip the chicken thighs once.
13. When cooking time is complete, open the lid and transfer the chicken thighs onto serving plates.
14. Serve hot.
15. Serving Suggestions: Enjoy with honey glazed baby carrots.
16. Variation Tip: Select the chicken thighs with a pinkish hue.

Nutrition:
- Info Calories: 413 Fat: 21g Sat Fat: 4.8g Carbohydrates: 4.1g Fiber: 0.1g Sugar: 2.8g Protein: 49.5g

Bang-bang Chicken

Servings: 6

Cooking Time: 15 Minutes

Ingredients:

- 1 oz. chicken breast tenderloins, small pieces
- ½ cup sweet chili sauce
- 1 cup of mayonnaise
- 1-1/2 cups bread crumbs
- 1/3 cup flour

Directions:

1. Whisk the sweet chili sauce and mayonnaise together in a bowl.

2. Spoon out 3 quarters of a cup from this. Set aside.

3. Keep flour in a plastic bag. Add the chicken and close this bag. Coat well by shaking.

4. Place the coated chicken in a large bowl with the mayonnaise mix.

5. Combine well by stirring.

6. Keep your bread crumbs in another plastic bag.

7. Place chicken pieces into the bread crumbs. Coat well.

8. Preheat your air fryer to 200 degrees C or 400 degrees F.

9. Transfer the chicken into the basket of your air fryer. Do not overcrowd.

10. Cook for 7 minutes.

11. Flip over and cook for another 4 minutes.

12. Transfer the chicken to a bowl. Pour over the reserved sauce.

13. You can also sprinkle some green onions before serving.

Nutrition:

- Info Calories 566, Carbohydrates 35g, Cholesterol 60mg, Total Fat 38g, Protein 21g, Sugar 7g, Fiber 1g, Sodium 818mg

Air Fryer Egg Rolls

Servings: 16
Cooking Time: 15 Minutes

Ingredients:
- 1 pack of egg roll wrappers
- 2 cups corn, thawed
- 1 can spinach, drained
- 1 can black beans, drained and rinsed
- 1 cup cheddar cheese, shredded

Directions:
1. Mix the corn, spinach, beans, Cheddar cheese, salt, and pepper in a bowl. This is for the filling.
2. Keep an egg roll wrapper.
3. Moisten lightly all the edges with your finger.
4. Keep a fourth of the filling at the wrapper's center.
5. Now fold a corner over the filling. Tuck the sides in to create a roll.
6. Repeat this process with the other wrappers.
7. Apply cooking spray on the egg rolls.
8. Preheat your air fryer at 199 degrees C or 390 degrees F.
9. Keep your egg rolls in its basket. They should not touch each other.
10. Fry for 7 minutes. Flip and cook for another 4 minutes.

Nutrition:
- Info Calories 260, Carbohydrates 27g, Cholesterol 25mg, Total Fat 12g, Protein 11g, Sugar 1g, Fiber 4g, Sodium 628mg

Glazed Turkey Breast

Servings: 10
Cooking Time: 55 Minutes

Ingredients:

- 1 teaspoon dried thyme, crushed
- ½ teaspoon dried sage, crushed
- ½ teaspoon smoked paprika
- Salt and freshly ground black pepper, to taste
- 1 (5-pound) boneless turkey breast
- 2 teaspoons olive oil
- ¼ cup maple syrup
- 2 tablespoons Dijon mustard
- 1 tablespoon butter, softened

Directions:

1. In a bowl, mix together the herbs, paprika, salt, and black pepper.
2. Coat the turkey breast with oil evenly.
3. Now, coat the outer side of turkey breast with herb mixture.
4. Press "Power Button" of Ninja Foodi Digital Air Fry Oven and turn the dial to select "Air Fry" mode.
5. Press "Time Button" and again turn the dial to set the cooking time to 55 minutes.
6. Now push "Temp Button" and rotate the dial to set the temperature at 350 degrees F.
7. Press "Start/Pause" button to start.
8. When the unit beeps to show that it is preheated, open the lid and grease the air fry basket.
9. Arrange the turkey breast into the prepared basket and insert in the oven.
10. While cooking, flip the turkey breast once after 25 minutes and then after 37 minutes.
11. Meanwhile, in a bowl, mix together the maple syrup, mustard, and butter.
12. After 50 minutes of cooking, press "Start/Pause" to pause cooking.
13. Remove the basket from Air Fryer and coat the turkey breast with glaze evenly.
14. Again, insert the basket in the oven and press "Start/Pause" to resume cooking.
15. When cooking time is complete, open the lid and place the turkey breast onto a cutting board for about 10 minutes before slicing.
16. With a sharp knife, cut the turkey breast into desired sized slices and serve.
17. Serving Suggestions: Green bean and goats cheese salad will be best for turkey meat.
18. Variation Tip: Place the turkey into the basket with the breast side down.

Nutrition:

- Info Calories: 30w, Fat: 3.3g, Sat Fat: 0.9g, Carbohydrates: 5.6g, Fiber: 0.2g Sugar: 4.7g, Protein: 26.2g

Nashville Chicken

Servings: 8
Cooking Time: 20 Minutes

Ingredients:
- 2 oz. chicken breast, boneless
- 2 tablespoons hot sauce
- ½ cup of olive oil
- 3 large eggs
- 3 cups all-purpose flour
- 1 teaspoon of chili powder
- 1-1/2 cups buttermilk

Directions:
1. Toss together the chicken, hot sauce, salt, and pepper in a bowl. Combine well.
2. Cover and refrigerate for three hours.
3. Pour flour into your bowl.
4. Now whisk the buttermilk and eggs together. Add 1 tablespoon of hot sauce.
5. For dredging your chicken, keep it in the flour first. Toss evenly for coating.
6. Keep it in your buttermilk mix. Then into the flour.
7. Keep them on your baking sheet.
8. Set the air fryer at 380 degrees. Place the tenders in your fryer.
9. Cook for 10 minutes.
10. For the sauce, whisk the spices and olive oil. Combine well.
11. Pour over the fried chicken immediately.

Nutrition:
- Info Calories 668, Carbohydrates 44g, Cholesterol 156mg, Total Fat 40g, Protein 33g, Sugar 5g, Fiber 2g, Sodium 847mg

Peruvian Chicken Drumsticks & Green Crema

Servings: 6

Cooking Time: 15 Minutes

Ingredients:

- 6 chicken drumsticks
- 2 garlic cloves, grated
- 1 tablespoon of olive oil
- 1 tablespoon honey
- 1 cup of baby spinach leaves, with stems removed
- ¼ cup cilantro leaves
- ¾ cup of sour cream

Directions:

1. Bring together the honey, garlic, pepper, and salt in a bowl.
2. Add the drumsticks. Coat well by tossing.
3. Keep the drumsticks in a vertical position in the basket. Keep them leaning against the wall of the basket.
4. Cook in your air fryer at 200 degrees C or 400 degrees F for 15 minutes.
5. In the meantime, combine the sour cream, cilantro leaves, pepper and salt in a food processor bowl.
6. Process until the crema has become smooth.
7. Drizzle the crema sauce over your drumsticks.

Nutrition:

- Info Calories 337, Carbohydrates 6g, Cholesterol 82mg, Total Fat 25g, Protein 22g, Sugar 3g, Fiber 0.5g, Sodium 574mg

Bacon-wrapped Chicken Breasts

Servings: 4
Cooking Time: 23 Minutes

Ingredients:

- 1 tablespoon palm sugar
- 6-7 Fresh basil leaves
- 2 tablespoons fish sauce
- 2 tablespoons water
- 2 (8-ounces) chicken breasts, cut each breast in half horizontally
- Salt and freshly ground black pepper, to taste
- 12 bacon strips
- 1½ teaspoon honey

Directions:

1. In a small heavy-bottomed pan, add palm sugar over medium-low heat and cook for about 2-3 minutes or until caramelized, stirring continuously.
2. Add the basil, fish sauce and water and stir to combine.
3. Remove from heat and transfer the sugar mixture into a large bowl.
4. Sprinkle each chicken breast with salt and black pepper.
5. Add the chicken pieces in the sugar mixture and coat generously.
6. Refrigerate to marinate for about 4-6 hours.
7. Wrap each chicken piece with 3 bacon strips.
8. Coat each piece with honey slightly.
9. Press "Power Button" of Ninja Foodi Digital Air Fry Oven and turn the dial to select "Air Fry" mode.
10. Press "Time Button" and again turn the dial to set the cooking time to 20 minutes.
11. Now push "Temp Button" and rotate the dial to set the temperature at 365 degrees F.
12. Press "Start/Pause" button to start.
13. When the unit beeps to show that it is preheated, open the lid and grease the air fry basket.
14. Arrange the chicken breasts into the prepared basket and insert in the oven.
15. Flip the chicken breasts once halfway through.
16. When cooking time is complete, open the lid and transfer the chicken breasts onto serving plates.
17. Serve hot.
18. Serving Suggestions: Serve with balsamic-glazed green beans.
19. Variation Tip: Use thick-cut bacon strips.

Nutrition:

- Info Calories: 709, Fat: 44.8g, Sat Fat: 14.3g, Carbohydrates: 6.8g, Fiber: 0g Sugar: 4.7g, Protein: 65.6g

BREAKFAST AND BRUNCH RECIPES

Baked Eggs

Servings: 4
Cooking Time: 12 Minutes

Ingredients:
- 1 cup marinara sauce, divided
- 1 tablespoon capers, drained and divided
- 8 eggs
- ¼ cup whipping cream, divided
- ¼ cup Parmesan cheese, shredded and divided
- Salt and ground black pepper, as required

Directions:
1. Grease 4 ramekins. Set aside.
2. Divide the marinara sauce in the bottom of each prepared ramekin evenly and top with capers.
3. Carefully, crack 2 eggs over marinara sauce into each ramekin and top with cream, followed by the Parmesan cheese.
4. Sprinkle each ramekin with salt and black pepper.
5. Press "Power Button" of Ninja Foodi Digital Air Fry Oven and turn the dial to select the "Air Bake" mode.
6. Press the Time button and again turn the dial to set the cooking time to 12 minutes.
7. Now push the Temp button and rotate the dial to set the temperature at 400 degrees F.
8. Press "Start/Pause" button to start.
9. When the unit beeps to show that it is preheated, open the lid.
10. Arrange the ramekins over the "Wire Rack" and insert in the oven.
11. Serve warm.

Nutrition:
- Info Calories 223 Total Fat 14.1 g Saturated Fat 5.5 g Cholesterol 341 mg Sodium 569 mg Total Carbs 9.8 g Fiber 1.7 g Sugar 6.2 g Protein 14.3 g

Spinach & Tomato Frittata

Servings: 6
Cooking Time: 30 Minutes

Ingredients:

- 10 large eggs
- Salt and freshly ground black pepper, to taste
- 1 (5-ounce) bag baby spinach
- 2 cups grape tomatoes, halved
- 4 scallions, sliced thinly
- 8 ounces feta cheese, crumbled
- 3 tablespoons hot olive oil

Directions:

1. In a bowl, place the eggs, salt and black pepper and beat well.
2. Add the spinach, tomatoes, scallions and feta cheese and gently stir to combine.
3. Spread the oil in a baking pan and top with the spinach mixture.
4. Press "Power Button" of Ninja Foodi Digital Air Fry Oven and turn the dial to select "Air Bake" mode.
5. Press "Time Button" and again turn the dial to set the cooking time to 30 minutes.
6. Now push "Temp Button" and rotate the dial to set the temperature at 350 degrees F.
7. Press "Start/Pause" button to start.
8. When the unit beeps to show that it is preheated, open the lid.
9. Arrange pan over the wire rack and insert in the oven.
10. When cooking time is complete, open the lid and place the pan aside for about 5 minutes.
11. Cut into equal-sized wedges and serve hot.
12. Serving Suggestions: Enjoy your frittata with garlicky potatoes.
13. Variation Tip: Pick the right cheese for frittata.

Nutrition:

- Info Calories: 298 Fat: 23.6g Sat Fat: 9.3g Carbohydrates: 6.1g Fiber: 1.5g Sugar: 4.1g Protein: 17.2g

Sausage Patties

Servings: 4
Cooking Time: 10 Minutes

Ingredients:
- 1 pack sausage patties
- 1 serving cooking spray

Directions:
1. Preheat your air fryer to 200 degrees C or 400 degrees F.
2. Keep the sausage patties in a basket. Work in batches if needed.
3. Cook for 3 minutes.
4. Turn the sausage over and cook for another 2 minutes.

Nutrition:
- Info Calories 168, Carbohydrates 1g, Cholesterol 46mg, Total Fat 12g, Protein 14g, Fiber 0g, Sodium 393mg, Sugars 1g

Roasted Cauliflower

Servings: 2

Cooking Time: 15 Minutes

Ingredients:
- 4 cups of cauliflower florets
- 1 tablespoon peanut oil
- 3 cloves garlic
- ½ teaspoon smoked paprika
- ½ teaspoon of salt

Directions:
1. Preheat your air fryer to 200 degrees C or 400 degrees F.
2. Now cut the garlic into half. Use a knife to smash it.
3. Keep in a bowl with salt, paprika, and oil.
4. Add the cauliflower. Coat well.
5. Transfer the coated cauliflower to your air fryer.
6. Cook for 10 minutes. Shake after 5 minutes.

Nutrition:
- Info Calories 136, Carbohydrates 12g, Cholesterol 0mg, Total Fat 8g, Protein 4g, Fiber 5.3g, Sodium 642mg, Sugars 5g

Cinnamon And Sugar Doughnuts

Servings: 9

Cooking Time: 16 Minutes

Ingredients:

- 1 teaspoon cinnamon
- 1/3 cup of white sugar
- 2 large egg yolks
- 2-1/2 tablespoons of butter, room temperature
- 1-1/2 teaspoons baking powder
- 2-1/4 cups of all-purpose flour

Directions:

1. Take a bowl and press your butter and white sugar together in it.
2. Add the egg yolks. Stir till it combines well.
3. Now sift the baking powder, flour, and salt in another bowl.
4. Keep one-third of the flour mix and half of the sour cream into your egg-sugar mixture. Stir till it combines well.
5. Now mix the remaining sour cream and flour. Refrigerate till you can use it.
6. Bring together the cinnamon and one-third sugar in your bowl.
7. Roll half-inch-thick dough.
8. Cut large slices (9) in this dough. Create a small circle in the center. This will make doughnut shapes.
9. Preheat your fryer to 175 degrees C or 350 degrees F.
10. Brush melted butter on both sides of your doughnut.
11. Keep half of the doughnuts in the air fryer's basket.
12. Apply the remaining butter on the cooked doughnuts.
13. Dip into the sugar-cinnamon mix immediately.

Nutrition:

- Info Calories 336, Carbohydrates 44g, Cholesterol 66mg, Total Fat 16g, Protein 4g, Fiber 1g, Sodium 390mg, Sugars 19g

Bell Pepper Omelet

Servings: 2
Cooking Time: 10 Minutes

Ingredients:

- 1 teaspoon butter
- 1 small onion, sliced
- ½ of green bell pepper, seeded and chopped
- 4 eggs
- ¼ teaspoon milk
- Salt and ground black pepper, as required
- ¼ cup Cheddar cheese, grated

Directions:

1. In a skillet, melt the butter over medium heat and cook the onion and bell pepper for about 4-5 minutes.
2. Remove the skillet from heat and set aside to cool slightly.
3. Meanwhile, in a bowl, add the eggs, milk, salt and black pepper and beat well.
4. Add the cooked onion mixture and gently, stir to combine.
5. Place the zucchini mixture into a small baking pan.
6. Press "Power Button" of Ninja Foodi Digital Air Fry Oven and turn the dial to select the "Air Fry" mode.
7. Press the Time button and again turn the dial to set the cooking time to 5 minutes.
8. Now push the Temp button and rotate the dial to set the temperature at 355 degrees F.
9. Press "Start/Pause" button to start.
10. When the unit beeps to show that it is preheated, open the lid.
11. Arrange pan over the "Wire Rack" and insert in the oven.
12. Cut the omelet into 2 portions and serve hot.

Nutrition:

- Info Calories 223 Total Fat 15.5 g Saturated Fat 6.9 g Cholesterol 347 mg Sodium 304 mg Total Carbs 6.4 g Fiber 1.2 g Sugar 3.8 g Protein 15.3 g

Tomato Quiche

Servings: 2
Cooking Time: 30 Minutes

Ingredients:

- 4 eggs
- ¼ cup onion, chopped
- ½ cup tomatoes, chopped
- ½ cup milk
- 1 cup Gouda cheese, shredded
- Salt, to taste

Directions:

1. In a small baking pan, add all the ingredients and mix well.
2. Press "Power Button" of Ninja Foodi Digital Air Fry Oven and turn the dial to select "Air Fry" mode.
3. Press "Time Button" and again turn the dial to set the cooking time to 30 minutes.
4. Now push "Temp Button" and rotate the dial to set the temperature at 340 degrees F.
5. Press "Start/Pause" button to start.
6. When the unit beeps to show that it is preheated, open the lid.
7. Arrange the pan over the wire rack and insert in the oven.
8. When cooking time is complete, open the lid and place the pan aside for about 5 minutes.
9. Cut into equal-sized wedges and serve.
10. Serving Suggestions: Fresh baby spring mix will be a great companion for this quiche.
11. Variation Tip: You can use any kind of fresh veggies for the filling of quiche.

Nutrition:

- Info Calories: 247 Fat: 16.1g Sat Fat: 7.5g Carbohydrates: 7.3g Fiber: 0.9g Sugar: 5.2g Protein: 18.6g

Eggs In Bread Cups

Servings: 4
Cooking Time: 23 Minutes

Ingredients:
- 4 bacon slices
- 2 bread slices, crust removed
- 4 eggs
- Salt and freshly ground black pepper, to taste

Directions:
1. Grease 4 cups of a muffin tin and set aside.
2. Heat a small frying pan over medium-high heat and cook the bacon slices for about 2-3 minutes.
3. With a slotted spoon, transfer the bacon slice onto a paper towel-lined plate to cool.
4. Break each bread slice in half.
5. Arrange 1 bread slices half in each of the prepared muffin cup and press slightly.
6. Now, arrange 1 bacon slice over each bread slice in a circular shape.
7. Crack 1 egg into each muffin cup and sprinkle with salt and black pepper.
8. Press "Power Button" of Ninja Foodi Digital Air Fry Oven and turn the dial to select "Air Bake" mode.
9. Press "Time Button" and again turn the dial to set the cooking time to 20 minutes.
10. Now push "Temp Button" and rotate the dial to set the temperature at 350 degrees F.
11. Press "Start/Pause" button to start.
12. When the unit beeps to show that it is preheated, open the lid.
13. Arrange the muffin tin over the wire rack and insert in the oven.
14. When cooking time is complete, open the lid and place the muffin tin onto a wire rack for about 10 minutes.
15. Serve warm.
16. Serving Suggestions: Feel free to top the bread cups with fresh herbs of your choice before serving.
17. Variation Tip: Pancetta can be used instead of bacon.

Nutrition:
- Info Calories: 98 Fat: 6.6g Sat Fat: 2.1g Carbohydrates: 2.6g Fiber: 0.1g Sugar: 0.5g Protein: 7.3g

Loaded Potatoes

Servings: 2
Cooking Time: 15 Minutes

Ingredients:
- 11 oz. baby potatoes
- 2 cut bacon slices
- 1-1/2 oz. low-fat cheddar cheese, shredded
- 1 teaspoon of olive oil
- 2 tablespoons low-fat sour cream

Directions:
1. Toss the potatoes with oil.
2. Place them in your air fryer basket. Cook till they get tender at 350°F. stir occasionally.
3. Cook the bacon meanwhile in a skillet till it gets crispy.
4. Take out the bacon from your pan. Crumble.
5. Keep the potatoes on a serving plate. Crush them lightly to split.
6. Top with cheese, chives, salt, crumbled bacon, and sour cream.

Nutrition:
- Info Calories 240, Carbohydrates 26g, Total Fat 12g, Protein 7g, Fiber 4g, Sodium 287mg, Sugars 3g

Cheese Toasts With Eggs & Bacon

Servings: 2
Cooking Time: 4 Minutes

Ingredients:

- 4 bread slices
- 1 garlic clove, minced
- 4 ounces goat cheese, crumbled
- Freshly ground black pepper, to taste
- 2 hard-boiled eggs, peeled and chopped
- 4 cooked bacon slices, crumbled

Directions:

1. In a food processor, add the garlic, ricotta, lemon zest and black pepper and pulse until smooth.
2. Spread ricotta mixture over each bread slices evenly.
3. Press "Power Button" of Ninja Foodi Digital Air Fry Oven and turn the dial to select the "Air Fry" mode.
4. Press the Time button and again turn the dial to set the cooking time to 4 minutes.
5. Now push the Temp button and rotate the dial to set the temperature at 355 degrees F.
6. Press "Start/Pause" button to start.
7. When the unit beeps to show that it is preheated, open the lid and lightly, grease the sheet pan.
8. Arrange the bread slices into "Air Fry Basket" and insert in the oven.
9. Top with egg and bacon pieces and serve.

Nutrition:

- Info Calories 416 Total Fat 29.2 g Saturated Fat 16.9 g Cholesterol 232 mg Sodium 531 mg Total Carbs 11.2 g Fiber 0.5 g Sugar 2.4 g Protein 27.2 g

Egg & Spinach Tart

Servings: 4

Cooking Time: 25 Minutes

Ingredients:

- 1 puff pastry sheet, trimmed into a 9x13-inch rectangle
- 4 eggs
- ½ cup cheddar cheese, grated
- 7 cooked thick-cut bacon strips
- ½ cup cooked spinach
- 1 egg, lightly beaten

Directions:

1. Arrange the pastry in a lightly greased "Sheet Pan".
2. With a small knife gently, cut a 1-inch border around the edges of the puff pastry without cutting all the way through.
3. With a fork, pierce the center of pastry a few times.
4. Press "Power Button" of Ninja Foodi Digital Air Fry Oven and turn the dial to select the "Air Bake" mode.
5. Press the Time button and again turn the dial to set the cooking time to 10 minutes.
6. Now push the Temp button and rotate the dial to set the temperature at 400 degrees F.
7. Press "Start/Pause" button to start.
8. When the unit beeps to show that it is preheated, open the lid.
9. Insert the "Sheet Pan" in the oven.
10. Remove the "Sheet Pan" from oven and sprinkle the cheese over the center.
11. Place the spinach and bacon in an even layer across the tart.
12. Now, crack the eggs, leaving space between each one.
13. Press "Power Button" of Ninja Foodi Digital Air Fry Oven and turn the dial to select the "Air Bake" mode.
14. Press the Time button and again turn the dial to set the cooking time to 15 minutes.
15. Now push the Temp button and rotate the dial to set the temperature at 400 degrees F.
16. Press "Start/Pause" button to start.
17. When the unit beeps to show that it is preheated, open the lid.
18. Insert the "Sheet Pan" in the oven.
19. Remove the "Sheet Pan" from oven and set aside to cool for 2-3 minutes before cutting.
20. With a pizza cutter, cut into4 portions and serve.

Nutrition:

- Info Calories 231 Total Fat 17.4 g Saturated Fat 8.2 g Cholesterol 236 mg Sodium 403 mg Total Carbs 5.7 g Fiber 0.3 g Sugar 0.8 g Protein 13.8 g

Bacon & Spinach Muffins

Servings: 6
Cooking Time: 17 Minutes

Ingredients:

- 6 eggs
- ½ cup milk
- Salt and freshly ground black pepper, to taste
- 1 cup fresh spinach, chopped
- 4 cooked bacon slices, crumbled

Directions:

1. In a bowl, add the eggs, milk, salt and black pepper and beat until well combined.
2. Add the spinach and stir to combine.
3. Divide the spinach mixture into 6 greased cups of an egg bite mold evenly.
4. Press "Power Button" of Ninja Foodi Digital Air Fry Oven and turn the dial to select "Air Fry" mode.
5. Press "Time Button" and again turn the dial to set the cooking time to 17 minutes.
6. Now push "Temp Button" and rotate the dial to set the temperature at 325 degrees F.
7. Press "Start/Pause" button to start.
8. When the unit beeps to show that it is preheated, open the lid.
9. Arrange the mold over the wire rack and insert in the oven.
10. When cooking time is complete, open the lid and place the mold onto a wire rack to cool for about 5 minutes.
11. Top with bacon pieces and serve warm.
12. Serving Suggestions: Serve these muffins with the drizzling of melted butter.
13. Variation Tip: Don't forget to grease the egg bite molds before pacing the egg mixture in them.

Nutrition:

- Info Calories: 179 Fat: 12.9g Sat Fat: 4.3g Carbohydrates: 1.8g Fiber: 0.1g Sugar: 1.3g Protein: 13.5g

French Toast Sticks

Servings: 2

Cooking Time: 10 Minutes

Ingredients:

- 4 slices of thick bread
- 2 eggs, lightly beaten
- 1 teaspoon cinnamon
- 1 teaspoon of vanilla extract
- ¼ cup milk

Directions:

1. Cut the bread into slices for making sticks.
2. Keep parchment paper on the air fryer basket's bottom.
3. Preheat your air fryer to 180 degrees C or 360 degrees F.
4. Now stir together the milk, eggs, cinnamon, vanilla extract, and nutmeg (optional). Combine well.
5. Dip each bread piece into the egg mix. Submerge well.
6. Remove the excess fluid by shaking it well.
7. Keep them in the fryer basket in a single layer.
8. Cook without overcrowding your fryer.

Nutrition:

- Info Calories 241, Carbohydrates 29g, Cholesterol 188mg, Total Fat 9g, Protein 11g, Fiber 2g, Sodium 423mg, Sugars 4g

Eggs In Avocado Cups

Servings: 2

Cooking Time: 10 Minutes

Ingredients:

- 1 avocado, halved and pitted
- 2 large eggs
- Salt and freshly ground black pepper, to taste
- 2 cooked bacon slices, crumbled

Directions:

1. Carefully scoop out about 2 teaspoons of flesh from each avocado half.
2. Crack 1 egg in each avocado half and sprinkle with salt and black pepper lightly.
3. Arrange avocado halves onto the greased piece of foil-lined sheet pan.
4. Press "Power Button" of Ninja Foodi Digital Air Fry Oven and turn the dial to select "Air Roast" mode.
5. Press "Time Button" and again turn the dial to set the cooking time to 10 minutes.
6. Now push "Temp Button" and rotate the dial to set the temperature at 375 degrees F.
7. Press "Start/Pause" button to start.
8. When the unit beeps to show that it is preheated, open the lid and insert the sheet pan in the oven.
9. When cooking time is complete, open the lid and transfer the avocado halves onto serving plates.
10. Top each avocado half with bacon pieces and serve.
11. Serving Suggestions: Serve these avocado halves with cherry tomatoes and fresh spinach.
12. Variation Tip: Smoked salmon can be replaced with bacon too.

Nutrition:

- Info Calories: 300 Fat: 26.6g Sat Fat: 6.4g Carbohydrates: 9g Fiber: 6.7g Sugar: 0.9g Protein: 9.7g

Tex-mex Hash Browns

Servings: 4

Cooking Time: 30 Minutes

Ingredients:

- 1-1/2 24 oz. potatoes, cut and peeled
- 1 onion, cut into small pieces
- 1 tablespoon of olive oil
- 1 jalapeno, seeded and cut
- 1 red bell pepper, seeded and cut

Directions:

1. Soak the potatoes in water.
2. Preheat your air fryer to 160 degrees C or 320 degrees F.
3. Drain and dry the potatoes using a clean towel.
4. Keep in a bowl.
5. Drizzle some olive oil over the potatoes, coat well.
6. Transfer to the air frying basket.
7. Add the onion, jalapeno, and bell pepper in the bowl.
8. Sprinkle half teaspoon olive oil, pepper, and salt. Coat well by tossing.
9. Now transfer your potatoes to the bowl with the veg mix from your fryer.
10. Place the empty basket into the air fryer. Raise the temperature to 180 degrees C or 356 degrees F.
11. Toss the contents of your bowl for mixing the potatoes with the vegetables evenly.
12. Transfer mix into the basket.
13. Cook until the potatoes have become crispy and brown.

Nutrition:

- Info Calories 197, Carbohydrates 34g, Cholesterol 0mg, Total Fat 5g, Protein 4g, Fiber 5g, Sodium 79mg, Sugars 3g

Ham & Hash Brown Casserole

Servings: 5
Cooking Time: 35 Minutes

Ingredients:

- 1½ tablespoons olive oil
- ½ of large onion, chopped
- 24 ounces frozen hash browns
- 3 eggs
- 2 tablespoons milk
- Salt and freshly ground black pepper, to taste
- ½ pound ham, chopped
- ¼ cup Cheddar cheese, shredded

Directions:

1. In a skillet, heat the oil over medium heat and sauté the onion for about 4-5 minutes.
2. Remove from the heat and transfer the onion into a bowl.
3. Add the hash browns and mix well.
4. Place the mixture into a baking pan.
5. Press "Power Button" of Ninja Foodi Digital Air Fry Oven and turn the dial to select "Air Bake" mode.
6. Press "Time Button" and again turn the dial to set the cooking time to 32 minutes.
7. Now push "Temp Button" and rotate the dial to set the temperature at 350 degrees F.
8. Press "Start/Pause" button to start.
9. When the unit beeps to show that it is preheated, open the lid.
10. Arrange pan over the wire rack and insert in the oven.
11. Stir the mixture once after 8 minutes.
12. Meanwhile, in a bowl, add the eggs, milk, salt and black pepper and beat well.
13. After 15 minutes of cooking, place the egg mixture over hash brown mixture evenly and top with the ham.
14. After 30 minutes of cooking, sprinkle the casserole with the cheese.
15. When cooking time is complete, open the lid and place the casserole dish aside for about 5 minutes.
16. Cut into equal-sized wedges and serve.
17. Serving Suggestions: Avocado slices will accompany this casserole greatly.
18. Variation Tip: Use freshly shredded cheese.

Nutrition:

- Info Calories: 540 Fat: 29.8g Sat Fat: 6.5g Carbohydrates: 51.5g Fiber: 5.3g Sugar: 3.2g Protein: 16.7g

FISH & SEAFOOD RECIPES

Blackened Fish Tacos

Servings: 4

Cooking Time: 15 Minutes

Ingredients:
- 1 oz. fillets of tilapia
- 1 can black beans, rinsed and drained
- 1 tablespoon olive oil
- 2 corn ears, cut the kernels
- 4 corn tortillas
- ¼ cup blackened seasoning

Directions:
1. Preheat your oven to 200 degrees C or 400 degrees F.
2. Bring together the corn, black beans, olive oil and salt in your bowl.
3. Stir gently until the corn and beans are coated evenly. Set aside.
4. Keep the fillets of fish on a work surface. Use paper towels to pat dry.
5. Apply cooking spray on each fillet lightly.
6. Sprinkle half of the blackened seasoning on the top.
7. Now flip over the fillets. Apply the cooking spray. Sprinkle the seasoning.
8. Keep the fish in your air fryer basket, in one single layer.
9. Cook for 2-3 minutes. Flip over and cook for another 2 minutes.
10. Take out and place on a plate.
11. Keep the corn and bean mix in the air fryer basket.
12. Cook for 8 minutes. Stir after 4 minutes.
13. Keep your fish in the corn tortillas. Apply the corn and bean mix on top.

Nutrition:
- Info Calories 376, Carbohydrates 43g, Cholesterol 42mg, Total Fat 8g, Protein 33g, Sugar 2g, Fiber 11g, Sodium 2210mg

Spiced Tilapia

Servings: 2
Cooking Time: 12 Minutes

Ingredients:

- ¼ teaspoon garlic powder
- ¼ teaspoon onion powder
- ¼ teaspoon ground cumin
- Salt and ground black pepper, as required
- 2 (6-ounce) tilapia fillets
- 1 tablespoon butter, melted

Directions:

1. In a small bowl, mix together the spices, salt and black pepper.
2. Coat the tilapia fillets with oil and then rub with spice mixture.
3. Press "Power Button" of Ninja Foodi Digital Air Fry Oven and turn the dial to select the "Air Fry" mode.
4. Press the Time button and again turn the dial to set the cooking time to 12 minutes.
5. Now push the Temp button and rotate the dial to set the temperature at 360 degrees F.
6. Press "Start/Pause" button to start.
7. When the unit beeps to show that it is preheated, open the lid.
8. Arrange the tilapia fillets over the greased "Wire Rack" and insert in the oven.
9. Flip the tilapia fillets once halfway through.
10. Serve hot.

Nutrition:

- Info Calories 194 Total Fat 7.4 g Saturated Fat 4.3 g Cholesterol 98 mg Sodium 179 mg Total Carbs 0.6 g Fiber 0.1 g Sugar 0.2 g Protein 31.8 g

Glazed Salmon

Servings: 2
Cooking Time: 8 Minutes

Ingredients:

- 2 (6-ounce) salmon fillets
- Salt, to taste
- 2 tablespoons honey

Directions:

1. Sprinkle the salmon fillets with salt and then coat with honey.
2. Press "Power Button" of Ninja Foodi Digital Air Fry Oven and turn the dial to select "Air Fry" mode.
3. Press "Time Button" and again turn the dial to set the cooking time to 8 minutes.
4. Now push "Temp Button" and rotate the dial to set the temperature at 355 degrees F.
5. Press "Start/Pause" button to start.
6. When the unit beeps to show that it is preheated, open the lid and grease the air fry basket.
7. Arrange the salmon fillets into the prepared air fry basket and insert in the oven.
8. When cooking time is complete, open the lid and transfer the salmon fillets onto serving plates.
9. Serve hot.
10. Serving Suggestions: Fresh baby greens will be great if served with glazed salmon.
11. Variation Tip: honey can be replaced with maple syrup too.

Nutrition:

- Info Calories: 289 Fat: 10.5g Sat Fat: 1.5g Carbohydrates: 17.3g Fiber: 0g Sugar: 17.3g Protein: 33.1g

Sweet & Tangy Herring

Servings: 2

Cooking Time: 12 Minutes

Ingredients:

- 2 (5-ounce) herring fillets
- 1 garlic clove, minced
- 1 teaspoon fresh rosemary, minced
- 1 tablespoon butter, melted
- 1 tablespoon balsamic vinegar
- ¼ teaspoon maple syrup
- 1/8 teaspoon Sriracha

Directions:

1. In a large resealable bag, place all the ingredients and seal the bag.
2. Shake the bag well to mix.
3. Place the bag in the refrigerator to marinate for at least 30 minutes.
4. Remove the fish fillets from bag and shake off the excess marinade.
5. Arrange the fish fillets onto the greased sheet pan in a single layer.
6. Press "Power Button" of Ninja Foodi Digital Air Fry Oven and turn the dial to select "Air Bake" mode.
7. Press "Time Button" and again turn the dial to set the cooking time to 12 minutes.
8. Now push "Temp Button" and rotate the dial to set the temperature at 450 degrees F.
9. Press "Start/Pause" button to start.
10. When the unit beeps to show that it is preheated, open the lid and insert the sheet pan in the oven.
11. Flip the fillets once halfway through.
12. When cooking time is complete, open the lid and transfer the fillets onto serving plates.
13. Serve hot.
14. Serving Suggestions: Enjoy with grilled vegetables.
15. Variation Tip: Use unsalted butter.

Nutrition:

- Info Calories: 347 Fat: 22.3g Sat Fat: 7.4g Carbohydrates: 1.6g Fiber: 0.3g Sugar: 0.5g Protein: 32.8g

Ranch Tilapia

Servings: 4
Cooking Time: 13 Minutes

Ingredients:

- ¾ cup cornflakes, crushed
- 1 (1-ounce) packet dry ranch-style dressing mix
- 2½ tablespoons vegetable oil
- 2 eggs
- 4 (6-ounce) tilapia fillets

Directions:

1. In a shallow bowl, crack the eggs and beat slightly.
2. In another bowl, add the cornflakes, ranch dressing, and oil and mix until a crumbly mixture forms.
3. Dip the fish fillets into egg and then, coat with the breadcrumbs mixture.
4. Press "Power Button" of Ninja Foodi Digital Air Fry Oven and turn the dial to select "Air Fry" mode.
5. Press "Time Button" and again turn the dial to set the cooking time to 13 minutes.
6. Now push "Temp Button" and rotate the dial to set the temperature at 356 degrees F.
7. Press "Start/Pause" button to start.
8. When the unit beeps to show that it is preheated, open the lid and grease the air fry basket.
9. Arrange the tilapia fillets into the prepared air fry basket and insert in the oven. When cooking time is complete, open the lid and transfer the fillets onto serving plates.
10. Serve hot.
11. Serving Suggestions: Serve tilapia with lemon butter.
12. Variation Tip: The skin should be removed, either before cooking or before serving.

Nutrition:

- Info Calories: 267 Fat: 12.2g Sat Fat: 3g Carbohydrates: 5.1g Fiber: 0.2g Sugar: 0.9g Protein: 34.9g

Lobster Tails With Garlic Butter-lemon

Servings: 2

Cooking Time: 10 Minutes

Ingredients:

- 2 lobster tails
- 1 teaspoon lemon zest
- 4 tablespoons of butter
- 1 garlic clove, grated
- 2 wedges of lemon

Directions:

1. Butterfly the lobster tails. Use kitchen shears to cut by length through the top shell's center and the meat.
2. Cut to the bottom portion of the shells.
3. Now spread halves of the tail apart.
4. Keep these tails in the basket of your air fry. The lobster meat should face up.
5. Melt the butter in your saucepan.
6. Add the garlic and lemon zest. Heat for 30 seconds.
7. Transfer two tablespoons of this mix to a bowl.
8. Brush on your lobster tails. Remove the remaining brushed butter.
9. Season with pepper and salt.
10. Cook in your air fryer at 195 degrees C or 380 degrees F. The lobster meat should turn opaque in about 5 or 7 minutes.
11. Apply the reserved butter over the lobster meat.
12. You can serve with lemon wedges.

Nutrition:

- Info Calories 462, Carbohydrates 3g, Cholesterol 129mg, Total Fat 42g, Protein 18g, Sugar 0g, Fiber 1g, Sodium 590mg

Crumbed Fish

Servings: 4
Cooking Time: 12 Minutes

Ingredients:

- 4 flounder fillets
- 1 cup bread crumbs
- 1 egg, beaten
- ¼ cup of vegetable oil
- 1 lemon, sliced

Directions:

1. Preheat your air fryer to 180 degrees C or 350 degrees F.
2. Mix the oil and bread crumbs in a bowl. Keep stirring until you see this mixture becoming crumbly and loose.
3. Now dip your fish fillets into the egg. Remove any excess.
4. Dip your fillets into the bread crumb mix. Make sure to coat evenly.
5. Keep the coated fillets in your preheated fryer gently.
6. Cook until you see the fish flaking easily with a fork.
7. Add lemon slices for garnishing.

Nutrition:

- Info Calories 389, Carbohydrates 23g, Cholesterol 107mg, Total Fat 21g, Protein 27g, Fiber 3g, Sodium 309mg, Sugars 2g

Cod Parcel

Servings: 2
Cooking Time: 15 Minutes

Ingredients:

- 2 tablespoons butter, melted
- 1 tablespoon fresh lemon juice
- ½ teaspoon dried tarragon
- Salt and freshly ground black pepper, to taste
- ½ cup red bell peppers, seeded and thinly sliced
- ½ cup carrots, peeled and julienned
- ½ cup fennel bulbs, julienned
- 2 (5-ounce) frozen cod fillets, thawed
- 1 tablespoon olive oil

Directions:

1. In a large bowl, mix together the butter, lemon juice, tarragon, salt, and black pepper.
2. Add the bell pepper, carrot, and fennel bulb and generously coat with the mixture.
3. Arrange 2 large parchment squares onto a smooth surface.
4. Coat the cod fillets with oil and then sprinkle evenly with salt and black pepper.
5. Arrange 1 cod fillet onto each parchment square and top each evenly with the vegetables.
6. Top with any remaining sauce from the bowl.
7. Fold the parchment paper and crimp the sides to secure fish and vegetables.
8. Press "Power Button" of Ninja Foodi Digital Air Fry Oven and turn the dial to select "Air Fry" mode.
9. Press "Time Button" and again turn the dial to set the cooking time to 15 minutes.
10. Now push "Temp Button" and rotate the dial to set the temperature at 350 degrees F.
11. Press "Start/Pause" button to start.
12. When the unit beeps to show that it is preheated, open the lid.
13. Arrange the cod parcels into the air fry basket and insert in the oven.
14. When cooking time is complete, open the lid and transfer the cod parcels onto serving plates.
15. Carefully open the parcels and serve hot.
16. Serving Suggestions: Serve with the drizzling of lime juice.
17. Variation Tip: You can use veggies of your choice.

Nutrition:

- Info Calories: 306 Fat: 20g Sat Fat: 8.4g Carbohydrates: 6.8g Fiber: 1.8g Sugar: 3g Protein: 26.3g

Seasoned Catfish

Servings: 4
Cooking Time: 23 Minutes

Ingredients:

- 4 (4-ounce) catfish fillets
- 2 tablespoons Italian seasoning
- Salt and freshly ground black pepper, to taste
- 1 tablespoon olive oil
- 1 tablespoon fresh parsley, chopped

Directions:

1. Rub the fish fillets with seasoning, salt and black pepper generously and then coat with oil.
2. Press "Power Button" of Ninja Foodi Digital Air Fry Oven and turn the dial to select "Air Fry" mode.
3. Press "Time Button" and again turn the dial to set the cooking time to 20 minutes.
4. Now push "Temp Button" and rotate the dial to set the temperature at 400 degrees F.
5. Press "Start/Pause" button to start.
6. When the unit beeps to show that it is preheated, open the lid and grease the air fry basket.
7. Arrange the fish fillets into the prepared air fry basket and insert in the oven.
8. Flip the fish fillets once halfway through.
9. When cooking time is complete, open the lid and transfer the fillets onto serving plates.
10. Serve hot with the garnishing of parsley.
11. Serving Suggestions: Quinoa salad will be a great choice for serving.
12. Variation Tip: Season the fish according to your choice.

Nutrition:

- Info Calories: 205 Fat: 14.2g Sat Fat: 2.4g Carbohydrates: 0.8g Fiber: 0g Sugar: 0.6g Protein: 17.7g

Crusted Salmon

Servings: 2
Cooking Time: 15 Minutes

Ingredients:

- 2 (6-ounce) skinless salmon fillets
- Salt and ground black pepper, as required
- 3 tablespoons walnuts, chopped finely
- 3 tablespoons quick-cooking oats, crushed
- 2 tablespoons olive oil

Directions:

1. Rub the salmon fillets with salt and black pepper evenly.
2. In a bowl, mix together the walnuts, oats and oil.
3. Arrange the salmon fillets onto the greased "Sheet Pan" in a single layer.
4. Place the oat mixture over salmon fillets and gently, press down.
5. Press "Power Button" of Ninja Foodi Digital Air Fry Oven and turn the dial to select the "Air Bake" mode.
6. Press the Time button and again turn the dial to set the cooking time to 15 minutes.
7. Now push the Temp button and rotate the dial to set the temperature at 400 degrees F.
8. Press "Start/Pause" button to start.
9. When the unit beeps to show that it is preheated, open the lid.
10. Insert the "Sheet Pan" in oven.
11. Serve hot.

Nutrition:

- Info Calories 446 Total Fat 31.9 g Saturated Fat 4 g Cholesterol 75 mg Sodium 153 mg Total Carbs 6.4 g Fiber 1.6 g Sugar 0.2 g Protein 36.8 g

Pesto Salmon

Servings: 4
Cooking Time: 15 Minutes

Ingredients:

- 1¼ pound salmon fillet, cut into 4 fillets
- 2 tablespoons white wine
- 1 tablespoon fresh lemon juice
- 2 tablespoons pesto, thawed
- 2 tablespoons pine nuts, toasted

Directions:

1. Arrange the salmon fillets onto q foil-lined baking pan, skin-side down.
2. Drizzle the salmon fillets with wine and lemon juice.
3. Set aside for about 15 minutes.
4. Spread pesto over each salmon fillet evenly.
5. Press "Power Button" of Ninja Foodi Digital Air Fry Oven and turn the dial to select the "Air Broil" mode.
6. Press the Time button and again turn the dial to set the cooking time to 15 minutes.
7. Press "Start/Pause" button to start.
8. When the unit beeps to show that it is preheated, open the lid.
9. Insert the baking pan in oven.
10. Garnish with toasted pine nuts and serve.

Nutrition:

- Info Calories 257 Total Fat 15 g Saturated Fat 2.1 g Cholesterol 64 mg Sodium 111 mg Total Carbs 1.3 g Fiber 0.3 g Sugar 0.8 g Protein 28.9 g

Buttered Trout

Servings: 2
Cooking Time: 10 Minutes

Ingredients:

- 2 (6-ounces) trout fillets
- Salt and ground black pepper, as required
- 1 tablespoon butter, melted

Directions:

1. Season each trout fillet with salt and black pepper and then, coat with the butter.
2. Arrange the trout fillets onto the greased "Sheet Pan" in a single layer.
3. Press "Power Button" of Ninja Foodi Digital Air Fry Oven and turn the dial to select the "Air Fry" mode.
4. Press the Time button and again turn the dial to set the cooking time to 10 minutes.
5. Now push the Temp button and rotate the dial to set the temperature at 360 degrees F.
6. Press "Start/Pause" button to start.
7. When the unit beeps to show that it is preheated, open the lid.
8. Insert the "Sheet Pan" in oven.
9. Flip the fillets once halfway through.
10. Serve hot.

Nutrition:

- Info Calories 374 Total Fat 20.2 g Saturated Fat 6.2 g Cholesterol 141 mg Sodium 232 mg Total Carbs 0 g Fiber 0 g Sugar 0 g Protein 45.4 g

Fish Sticks

Servings: 4
Cooking Time: 10 Minutes

Ingredients:

- 16 oz. fillets of tilapia or cod
- 1 egg
- ¼ cup all-purpose flour
- ¼ cup Parmesan cheese, grated
- 1 teaspoon of paprika
- ½ cup bread crumbs

Directions:

1. Preheat your air fryer to 200 degrees C or 400 degrees F.
2. Use paper towels to pat dry your fish.
3. Cut into 1 x 3-inch sticks.
4. Keep flour in a dish. Beat the egg in another dish.
5. Bring together the paprika, cheese, bread crumbs and some pepper in another shallow dish.
6. Coat the sticks of fish in flour.
7. Now dip them in the egg and coat the bread crumbs mix.
8. Apply cooking spray on the air fryer basket.
9. Keep the sticks in your basket. They shouldn't touch.
10. Apply cooking spray on each fish stick.
11. Cook in the air fryer for 3 minutes. Flip over and cook for another 2 minutes.

Nutrition:

- Info Calories 217, Carbohydrates 17g, Cholesterol 92mg, Total Fat 5g, Protein 26g, Fiber 0.7g, Sugar 0g, Sodium 245mg

Lemony Shrimp

Servings: 3
Cooking Time: 8 Minutes

Ingredients:

- 2 tablespoons fresh lemon juice
- 1 tablespoon olive oil
- 1 teaspoon lemon pepper
- ¼ teaspoon paprika
- ¼ teaspoon garlic powder
- 12 ounces medium shrimp, peeled and deveined

Directions:

1. In a large bowl, add all the ingredients except the shrimp and mix until well combined.
2. Add the shrimp and toss to coat well.
3. Arrange the shrimps onto a sheet pan.
4. Press "Power Button" of Ninja Foodi Digital Air Fry Oven and turn the dial to select "Air Fry" mode.
5. Press "Time Button" and again turn the dial to set the cooking time to 8 minutes.
6. Now push "Temp Button" and rotate the dial to set the temperature at 400 degrees F.
7. Press "Start/Pause" button to start.
8. When the unit beeps to show that it is preheated, open the lid and insert the sheet pan in the oven.
9. When cooking time is complete, open the lid and transfer the shrimp onto serving plates.
10. Serve hot.
11. Serving Suggestions: Serve with scalloped potatoes.
12. Variation Tip: Avoid shrimp that smell like ammonia.

Nutrition:

- Info Calories: 164 Fat: 6.1g Sat Fat: 0.8g Carbohydrates: 0.9g Fiber: 0.3g Sugar: 0.3g Protein: 24.5g

Halibut & Shrimp With Pasta

Servings: 4
Cooking Time: 10 Minutes

Ingredients:

- 14 ounces pasta
- 4 tablespoons pesto, divided
- 4 (4-ounce) halibut steaks
- 2 tablespoons olive oil
- ½ pound tomatoes, chopped
- 8 large shrimp, peeled and deveined
- 2 tablespoons fresh lime juice
- 2 tablespoons fresh dill, chopped

Directions:

1. In the bottom of a baking pan, spread 1 tablespoon of pesto.
2. Place halibut steaks and tomatoes over pesto in a single layer and drizzle with the oil.
3. Now, place the shrimp on top in a single layer.
4. Drizzle with lime juice and sprinkle with dill.
5. Press "Power Button" of Ninja Foodi Digital Air Fry Oven and turn the dial to select "Air Fry" mode.
6. Press "Time Button" and again turn the dial to set the cooking time to 8 minutes.
7. Now push "Temp Button" and rotate the dial to set the temperature at 390 degrees F.
8. Press "Start/Pause" button to start.
9. When the unit beeps to show that it is preheated, open the lid.
10. Place the pan over the wire rack and insert in the oven.
11. Meanwhile, in a large pan of salted boiling water, add the pasta and cook for about 8-10 minutes or until desired doneness.
12. Drain the pasta and transfer into a large bowl.
13. Add the remaining pesto and toss to coat well.
14. When cooking time is complete, open the lid and divide the pasta onto serving plates.
15. Top with the fish mixture and serve immediately.
16. Serving Suggestions: Serve with the topping of freshly grated Parmesan.
17. Variation Tip: Linguine pasta will be the best choice for this recipe.

Nutrition:

- Info Calories: 606 Fat: 19.4g Sat Fat: 3.2g Carbohydrates: 59.1g Fiber: 1.1g Sugar: 2.5g Protein: 47.4g

SNACK & DESSERT RECIPES

Sugared Grapefruit

Servings: 2

Cooking Time: 5 Minutes

Ingredients:

- 2 tablespoons granulated sugar
- 2 teaspoons brown sugar
- 1 large grapefruit, halved
- Pinch of flaky sea salt

Directions:

1. In a small bowl, mix together both sugars.
2. Arrange the grapefruit halves onto the greased "Sheet Pan" cut sides up and sprinkle with sugar mixture.
3. Press "Power Button" of Ninja Foodi Digital Air Fry Oven and turn the dial to select the "Air Broil" mode.
4. Press the Time button and again turn the dial to set the cooking time to 5 minutes.
5. Press "Start/Pause" button to start.
6. When the unit beeps to show that it is preheated, open the lid.
7. Insert the "Sheet Pan" in oven.
8. Sprinkle with sea salt and serve.

Nutrition:

- Info Calories 77 Total Fat 0.1 g Saturated Fat 0 g Cholesterol 0 mg Sodium 118 mg Total Carbs 20.1 g Fiber 0.7 g Sugar 19.4 g Protein 0.4 g

Air Fryer Beignets

Servings: 7
Cooking Time: 15 Minutes

Ingredients:

- ½ cup all-purpose flour
- 1 egg, separated
- ½ teaspoon of baking powder
- 1-1/2 teaspoons melted butter
- ¼ cup white sugar
- ½ teaspoon of vanilla extract

Directions:

1. Preheat your air fryer to 185 degrees C or 370 degrees F.
2. Whisk together the sugar, flour, butter, egg yolk, vanilla extract, baking powder, salt, and water in a bowl. Combine well by stirring.
3. Use an electric hand mixer to beat the white portion of the egg in a bowl.
4. Fold this into the batter.
5. Now use a small ice cream scoop to add the mold.
6. Keep the mold into the air fryer basket.
7. Fry for 10 minutes in your air fryer.
8. Take out the mold and the pop beignets carefully.
9. Flip them over on a round of parchment paper.
10. Now transfer the parchment round with the beignets into the fryer basket.
11. Cook for 4 more minutes.

Nutrition:

- Info Calories 99, Carbohydrates 16g, Cholesterol 29mg, Total Fat 3g, Protein 2g, Sugar 9g, Fiber 0.2g, Sodium 74mg

French Fries

Servings: 4
Cooking Time: 30 Minutes

Ingredients:

- 1 pound potatoes, peeled and cut into strips
- 3 tablespoons olive oil
- ½ teaspoon onion powder
- ½ teaspoon garlic powder
- 1 teaspoon paprika

Directions:

1. In a large bowl of water, soak the potato strips for about 1 hour.
2. Drain the potato strips well and pat them dry with paper towels.
3. In a large bowl, add the potato strips and the remaining ingredients and toss to coat well.
4. Press "Power Button" of Ninja Foodi Digital Air Fry Oven and turn the dial to select "Air Fry" mode.
5. Press "Time Button" and again turn the dial to set the cooking time to 30 minutes.
6. Now push "Temp Button" and rotate the dial to set the temperature at 375 degrees F.
7. Press "Start/Pause" button to start.
8. When the unit beeps to show that it is preheated, open the lid.
9. Arrange the potato fries into the air fry basket and insert in the oven.
10. When cooking time is complete, open the lid and transfer the fries onto a platter.
11. Serve warm.
12. Serving Suggestions: Serve these fries with ketchup.
13. Variation Tip: Choose starchy potatoes for fries.

Nutrition:

- Info Calories: 172 Fat: 10.7g Sat Fat: 1.5g Carbohydrates: 18.6g Fiber: 3g Sugar: 1.6g Protein: 2.1g

Chicken Wings

Servings: 4
Cooking Time: 25 Minutes

Ingredients:
- 1½ pounds chicken wingettes and drumettes
- 1/3 cup tomato sauce
- 2 tablespoons balsamic vinegar
- 2 tablespoons maple syrup
- ½ teaspoon liquid smoke
- ¼ teaspoon red pepper flakes, crushed
- Salt, as required

Directions:
1. Arrange the wings onto the greased "Sheet Pan".
2. Place the tofu mixture in the greased "Sheet Pan".
3. Press "Power Button" of Ninja Foodi Digital Air Fry Oven and turn the dial to select the "Air Fry" mode.
4. Press the Time button and again turn the dial to set the cooking time to 25 minutes.
5. Now push the Temp button and rotate the dial to set the temperature at 380 degrees F.
6. Press "Start/Pause" button to start.
7. When the unit beeps to show that it is preheated, open the lid.
8. Insert the "Sheet Pan" in oven.
9. Meanwhile, in a small pan, add the remaining ingredients over medium heat and cook for about 10 minutes, stirring occasionally.
10. Remove from oven and place the chicken wings into a bowl.
11. Add the sauce and toss to coat well.
12. Serve immediately.

Nutrition:
- Info Calories 356 Total Fat 12.7 g Saturated Fat 3.5 g Cholesterol 151 mg Sodium 293 mg Total Carbs 7.9 g Fiber 0.3 g Sugar 6.9 g Protein 49.5 g

Beef Taquitos

Servings: 6
Cooking Time: 8 Minutes

Ingredients:

- 6 corn tortillas
- 2 cups cooked beef, shredded
- ½ cup onion, chopped
- 1 cup pepper jack cheese, shredded
- Olive oil cooking spray

Directions:

1. Arrange the tortillas onto a smooth surface.
2. Place the shredded meat over one corner of each tortilla, followed by onion and cheese.
3. Roll each tortilla to secure the filling and secure with toothpicks.
4. Spray each taquito with cooking spray evenly.
5. Arrange the taquitos onto the greased "Sheet Pan".
6. Place the tofu mixture in the greased "Sheet Pan".
7. Press "Power Button" of Ninja Foodi Digital Air Fry Oven and turn the dial to select the "Air Fry" mode.
8. Press the Time button and again turn the dial to set the cooking time to 8 minutes.
9. Now push the Temp button and rotate the dial to set the temperature at 400 degrees F.
10. Press "Start/Pause" button to start.
11. When the unit beeps to show that it is preheated, open the lid.
12. Insert the "Sheet Pan" in oven.
13. Serve warm.

Nutrition:

- Info Calories 228 Total Fat 9.6 g Saturated Fat 4.8 g Cholesterol 67 mg Sodium 235 mg Total Carbs 12.3 g Fiber 1.7 g Sugar 0.6 g Protein 22.7 g

Plum Crisp

Servings: 2
Cooking Time: 40 Minutes

Ingredients:

- 1½ cups plums, pitted and sliced
- ¼ cup sugar, divided
- 1½ teaspoons cornstarch
- 3 tablespoons flour
- ¼ teaspoon ground cinnamon
- Pinch of salt
- 1½ tablespoons cold butter, chopped
- 3 tablespoons rolled oats

Directions:

1. In a bowl, place plum slices, 1 teaspoon of sugar and cornstarch and toss to coat well.
2. Divide the plum mixture into lightly greased 2 (8-ounce) ramekins.
3. In a bowl, mix together the flour, remaining sugar, cinnamon and salt.
4. With a pastry blender, cut in bitterer until a crumbly mixture forms.
5. Add the oats and gently stir to combine.
6. Place the oat mixture over plum slices into each ramekin.
7. Press "Power Button" of Ninja Foodi Digital Air Fry Oven and turn the dial to select "Air Bake" mode.
8. Press "Time Button" and again turn the dial to set the cooking time to 40 minutes.
9. Now push "Temp Button" and rotate the dial to set the temperature at 350 degrees F.
10. Press "Start/Pause" button to start.
11. When the unit beeps to show that it is preheated, open the lid.
12. Arrange the ramekins over the wire rack and insert in the oven.
13. When cooking time is complete, open the lid and place the ramekins onto a wire rack to cool for about 10 minutes.
14. Serve warm.
15. Serving Suggestions: Vanilla ice cream will go great with crisp.
16. Variation Tip: Select plums with a sweet aroma and free of bruises and faded spots.

Nutrition:

- Info Calories: 273 Fat: 9.4g Sat Fat: 5.6g Carbohydrates: 47.2g Fiber: 1.9g Sugar: 30.4g Protein: 2.7g

Sugar And Cinnamon Doughnuts

Servings: 9

Cooking Time: 16 Minutes

Ingredients:

- 2 egg yolks
- 1-1/2 teaspoons baking powder
- 2-1/4 cups of all-purpose flour
- 2 tablespoons of butter
- ½ cup of white sugar
- ½ cup sour cream

Directions:

1. Press butter and ½ cup of white sugar together in a bowl. It should get crumbly.
2. Add the egg yolks. Stir to combine well.
3. Now sift baking powder, flour, and salt into another bowl.
4. Place a third of the flour mix and half sour cream into your egg-sugar mix.
5. Combine well by stirring.
6. Mix the remaining sour cream and flour in.
7. Refrigerate this dough until you can use it.
8. Now mix 1/3rd cup of sugar.
9. Roll your dough to half-inch thickness on a work surface.
10. Cut the dough into 9 circles. Create a small circle at the center of each circle. The shape should be like a doughnut.
11. Preheat your air fryer to 175 degrees C or 350 degrees F.
12. Brush half of the melted butter on both sides of your doughnut.
13. Transfer half of the doughnuts into your air fryer basket.
14. Cook for 6 minutes. Apply melted butter on the doughnuts.

Nutrition:

- Info Calories 336, Carbohydrates 44g, Cholesterol 66mg, Total Fat 16g, Protein 4g, Sugar 19g, Fiber 1g, Sodium 390mg

Gluten-free Cherry Crumble

Servings: 4

Cooking Time: 25 Minutes

Ingredients:

- 3 cups pitted cherries
- 2 teaspoons of lemon juice
- 1/3 cup butter
- 1 cup gluten-free all-purpose baking flour
- 1 teaspoon vanilla powder
- 10 tablespoons of white sugar

Directions:

1. Cube the butter and refrigerate for about 15 minutes. It should get firm.
2. Preheat your air fryer to 165 degrees C or 325 degrees F.
3. Bring together the pitted cherries, lemon juice, and 2 tablespoons of sugar in your bowl. Mix well.
4. Pour the cherry mix into a baking dish.
5. Now mix 6 tablespoons of sugar and flour in a bowl.
6. Use your fingers to cut in the butter. Particles should be pea-size.
7. Keep them over the cherries. Press down lightly.
8. Stir in the vanilla powder and 2 tablespoons of sugar in your bowl.
9. Dust the sugar topping over flour and cherries.
10. Transfer to your air fryer and bake.
11. Leave it inside for 10 minutes once the baking is done.
12. Set aside for 5 minutes to cool.

Nutrition:

- Info Calories 576, Carbohydrates 76g, Cholesterol 41mg, Total Fat 28g, Protein 5g, Sugar 49g, Fiber 6g, Sodium 109mg

Mozzarella Sticks

Servings: 4
Cooking Time: 15 Minutes

Ingredients:

- 1/3 cup all-purpose flour
- 1 tablespoon cornmeal
- 1-1/2 teaspoon of garlic powder
- 1 cup bread crumbs
- ¼ teaspoon onion powder
- ½ teaspoon flakes of parsley
- ¼ teaspoon oregano, dried

Directions:

1. Place flour, cornmeal, water, garlic powder, and salt in a bowl.
2. Mix to create a batter. Get the consistency of pancake batter.
3. Stir in the parsley, onion powder, bread crumbs, salt, and pepper in another shallow and wide bowl.
4. Coat flour on the mozzarella sticks lightly.
5. Dip the sticks in your batter. Toss the bread crumb mix in. Coat well.
6. Now keep the sticks in your baking sheet in one layer.
7. Refrigerate for an hour minimum.
8. Preheat your air fryer to 200 degrees C or 400 degrees F.
9. Keep the mozzarella sticks in your fryer basket. Apply cooking spray lightly.
10. Cook them for 5 minutes. Flip the sticks and cook for another 5 minutes.

Nutrition:

- Info Calories 307, Carbohydrates 39g, Cholesterol 23mg, Total Fat 11g, Protein 13g, Sugar 1g, Fiber 0.7g, Sodium 936mg

Wrapped Bacon Chicken Thighs

Servings: 4

Cooking Time: 25 Minutes

Ingredients:

- ½ garlic clove, minced
- ½ butter stick, softened
- ¼ teaspoon basil, dried
- 1-1/2 oz. chicken thighs, boneless and skinless
- 1/3 oz. bacon, thick-cut

Directions:

1. Combine the garlic, softened butter, pepper, salt, and basil in your bowl.
2. Take a wax paper piece and keep the butter on it.
3. Roll it up to create a butter log.
4. Refrigerate it until it becomes firm.
5. Lay a strip of bacon on a wax paper piece.
6. Keep your chicken thighs on the bacon's top. Sprinkle some garlic.
7. Now open your chicken thigh. Keep 1 to 2 teaspoons on cold butter at its middle.
8. Tuck an end of the bacon into the center of the thigh.
9. Fold this over the chicken. Roll your bacon around the thigh.
10. Preheat your air fryer to 190 degrees C or 370 degrees F.
11. Keep the chicken thighs in your air fryer basket.
12. Cook for 20 minutes. The chicken shouldn't be pink anymore. The juices should be running clear.

Nutrition:

- Info Calories 568, Carbohydrates 1g, Cholesterol 150mg, Total Fat 48g, Protein 33g, Sugar 0g, Fiber 0.2g, Sodium 441mg

Cheese Pastries

Servings: 6
Cooking Time: 10 Minutes

Ingredients:

- 1 egg yolk
- 4 ounces feta cheese, crumbled
- 1 scallion, finely chopped
- 2 tablespoons fresh parsley, finely chopped
- Salt and freshly ground black pepper, to taste
- 2 frozen phyllo pastry sheets, thawed
- 2 tablespoons olive oil

Directions:

1. In a large bowl, add the egg yolk, and beat well.
2. Add the feta cheese, scallion, parsley, salt, and black pepper and mix well.
3. Cut each pastry sheet in three strips.
4. Add about 1 teaspoon of feta mixture on the underside of a strip.
5. Fold the tip of the pastry sheet over the filling in a zigzag manner to form a triangle.
6. Repeat with the remaining strips and fillings.
7. Coat each pastry with oil evenly.
8. Press "Power Button" of Ninja Foodi Digital Air Fry Oven and turn the dial to select "Air Fry" mode.
9. Press "Time Button" and again turn the dial to set the cooking time to 3 minutes.
10. Now push "Temp Button" and rotate the dial to set the temperature at 390 degrees F.
11. Press "Start/Pause" button to start.
12. When the unit beeps to show that it is preheated, open the lid.
13. Arrange the pastries in the air fry basket and insert in the oven.
14. After 3 minutes, set the temperature at 390 degrees F for 2 minutes.
15. When cooking time is complete, open the lid and transfer the pastries onto a platter.
16. Serve warm.
17. Serving Suggestions: Serve these pastries with marinara sauce.
18. Variation Tip: Feta cheese can be replaced with ricotta cheese too.

Nutrition:

- Info Calories: 128 Fat: 10g Sat Fat: 3.9g Carbohydrates: 6g Fiber: 0.3g Sugar: 0.9g Protein: 3.9g

Vanilla Cheesecake

Servings: 6
Cooking Time: 14 Minutes

Ingredients:

- 1 cup honey graham cracker crumbs
- 2 tablespoons unsalted butter, softened
- 1 pound cream cheese, softened
- ½ cup sugar
- 2 large eggs

Directions:

1. Line a round baking pan with parchment paper.
2. For crust: in a bowl, add the graham cracker crumbs and butter.
3. Place the crust into the baking dish and press to smooth.
4. Press "Power Button" of Ninja Foodi Air Fry Oven and turn the dial to select the "Air Fry" mode.
5. Press "Time Button" and again turn the dial to set the cooking time to 4 minutes.
6. Now push "Temp Button" and rotate the dial to set the temperature at 350 degrees F.
7. Press "Start/Pause" button to start.
8. When the unit beeps to show that it is preheated, open the lid.
9. Arrange the baking pan of crust into the air fry basket and insert in the oven.
10. When cooking time is complete, open the lid and place the crust aside to cool for about 10 minutes.
11. Meanwhile, in a bowl, add the cream cheese and sugar and whisk until smooth.
12. Now, place the eggs, one at a time and whisk until the mixture becomes creamy.
13. Add the vanilla extract and mix well.
14. Place the cream cheese mixture over the crust evenly.
15. Press "Power Button" of Ninja Foodi Air Fry Oven and turn the dial to select the "Air Fry" mode.
16. Press "Time Button" and again turn the dial to set the cooking time to 10 minutes.
17. Now push "Temp Button" and rotate the dial to set the temperature at 350 degrees F.
18. Press "Start/Pause" button to start.
19. When the unit beeps to show that it is preheated, open the lid.
20. Arrange the baking pan into the air fry basket and insert in the oven.
21. When cooking time is complete, open the lid and place the pan onto a wire rack to cool completely.
22. Refrigerate overnight before serving.
23. Serving Suggestions: Serve with the topping of fresh berries.
24. Variation Tip: Your cream cheese should always be at room temperature.

Nutrition:

- Info Calories: 470 Fat: 33.9g, Sat Fat: 20.6g Carbohydrates: 349g, Fiber: 0.5g Sugar: 22g Protein: 9.4g

Banana Cake

Servings: 4
Cooking Time: 30 Minutes

Ingredients:

- 1 mashed banana
- 1 egg
- 1/3 cup brown sugar
- 3-1/2 tablespoons of butter, room temperature
- 1 cup flour
- 2 tablespoons of honey

Directions:

1. Preheat your air fryer to 160 degrees C or 320 degrees F.
2. Apply cooking spray on a small tube pan.
3. Beat the butter and sugar together in your bowl. It should turn creamy.
4. Bring together the egg, banana, and honey in another bowl.
5. Now whisk this banana mix into your butter mixture. It should be smooth.
6. Stir in the salt and flour into this mixture.
7. Mix the batter until it gets smooth.
8. Keep in the pan and transfer to the air fryer basket.
9. Bake until you see a toothpick coming out clean from the cake.

Nutrition:

- Info Calories 419, Carbohydrates 57g, Cholesterol 73mg, Total Fat 19g, Protein 5g, Sugar 30g, Fiber 2g, Sodium 531mg

Chili Dip

Servings: 8
Cooking Time: 15 Minutes

Ingredients:

- 1 (8-ounce) package cream cheese, softened
- 1 (16-ounce) can Hormel chili without beans
- 1 (16-ounce) package mild cheddar cheese, shredded

Directions:

1. In a baking pan, place the cream cheese and spread in an even layer.
2. Top with chili evenly, followed by the cheese.
3. Press "Power Button" of Ninja Foodi Digital Air Fry Oven and turn the dial to select "Air Bake" mode.
4. Press "Time Button" and again turn the dial to set the cooking time to 15 minutes.
5. Now push "Temp Button" and rotate the dial to set the temperature at 375 degrees F.
6. Press "Start/Pause" button to start.
7. When the unit beeps to show that it is preheated, open the lid.
8. Arrange pan over the wire rack and insert in the oven.
9. When cooking time is complete, open the lid.
10. Serve hot.
11. Serving Suggestions: serve this dip with tortilla chips or fresh veggies.
12. Variation Tip: Coby cheese can be replaced with cheddar cheese.

Nutrition:

- Info Calories: 388 Fat: 31.3g Sat Fat: 19.2g Carbohydrates: 5.6g Fiber: 0.7g Sugar: 1.1g Protein: 21.1g

Jalapeño Poppers

Servings: 6
Cooking Time: 13 Minutes

Ingredients:
- 12 large jalapeño peppers
- 8 ounces cream cheese, softened
- ¼ cup scallion, chopped
- ¼ cup fresh cilantro, chopped
- ¼ teaspoon onion powder
- ¼ teaspoon garlic powder
- Salt, to taste
- 1/3 cup sharp cheddar cheese, grated

Directions:
1. Carefully cut off one-third of each pepper lengthwise and then scoop out the seeds and membranes.
2. In a bowl, mix together the cream cheese, scallion, cilantro, spices and salt.
3. Stuff each pepper with the cream cheese mixture and top with cheese.
4. Arrange the jalapeño peppers onto the greased sheet pan.
5. Press "Power Button" of Ninja Foodi Digital Air Fry Oven and turn the dial to select "Air Fry" mode.
6. Press "Time Button" and again turn the dial to set the cooking time to 13 minutes.
7. Now push "Temp Button" and rotate the dial to set the temperature at 400 degrees F.
8. Press "Start/Pause" button to start.
9. When the unit beeps to show that it is preheated, open the lid and insert the sheet pan in the oven.
10. When cooking time is complete, open the lid and transfer the jalapeño poppers onto a platter.
11. Serve immediately.
12. Serving Suggestions:
13. Variation Tip:

Nutrition:
- Info Calories: 171 Fat: 15.7g Sat Fat: 9.7g Carbohydrates: 3.7g Fiber: 1.3g Sugar: 1.2g Protein: 4.9g

RECIPES INDEX